Senten

Diagramming

Beginning

Sentence Diagramming products available in print or eBook form.

Beginning • Level 1 • Level 2

Written by
Angela Carter

Graphic Design by
Mary O'Dell
Scott Slyter

Edited by
Patricia Gray

THE CRITICAL THINKING CO.™
www.CriticalThinking.com
Phone: 800-458-4849 • Fax: 541-756-1758
1991 Sherman Ave., Suite 200 • North Bend • OR 97459
ISBN 978-1-60144-853-8

Printed in the United States of America by McNaughton & Gunn, Inc., Saline, MI (Sept. 2020)

Table of Contents

About This Book

I began writing this series while teaching elementary children how to diagram sentences. I just couldn't find quality resources out there that laid out diagramming as a logical process, building on itself from simple subject-verb sentences up through complex sentences with dependent clauses—at least not for the younger crowd. I found myself making up sentences and planning quick lessons on my own, so I decided to write them down and share!

I first fell in love with sentence diagramming in college. Through elementary and middle school our grammar lessons had us "circle the adjective and draw a line from the adjective to the noun it modifies." I found this task to be messy and disorganized, lines crossing over each other squeezed between the words on the page. It was confusing to look at and made me grumpy. I was thrilled when, in "English Grammar 101," I learned to sort and organize all the words of a sentence onto lines, showing their relationships and the structure of the sentence! For me—and many other visual learners—this visual representation of the English language was very helpful!

During my career as an elementary and middle school teacher and private tutor I have seen many students labor over grammar exercises similar to the ones in my old grammar books. Students' handwriting is sloppy; their lines go all over the place; they can't find the direct object to save their lives. They are told to write a paragraph which includes at least two complex sentences with dependent clauses, yet they don't truly understand what a dependent clause or a subordinating conjunction is. I started thinking about how very visually-oriented students of the 21st century are and decided to bring back diagramming. My students were amazed at how fun diagramming actually can be. They found sense in the structure of a sentence and a clear and true sense of satisfaction with each completed diagram. Even the kids who were traditionally more "math minded" began to enjoy English lessons. One even called diagramming "the math of English class." They started asking how to diagram more and more complex sentences, looking for examples in the books they were reading, trying to stump me by composing the most complex sentences they could imagine. The grammar lessons were actually spilling over into the writing lessons!

I find the benefits of sentence diagramming to be multi-faceted. Students learn critical thinking skills in a way never presented to them before. They learn information organization skills, and how to make a visual representation of language. They begin to truly understand the finer points of English grammar. Their writing becomes more complex and mature. For many students, boring old grammar lessons become fun.

I hope you will find much success with *Sentence Diagramming: Beginning*. Please feel free to extend the lessons beyond what is written in this book. Find sentences to diagram from literature, magazines, your own conversations, and the students' own writings! Draw diagrams large, on marker boards, butcher paper, and poster boards. Embrace the "visual organization" of language—and most of all—have fun!

Lesson 1: Simple Subject and Main Verb

A simple sentence has a noun (subject) and a verb (predicate).

To diagram a sentence, start with a main line that has a vertical (subject/predicate) line through it.

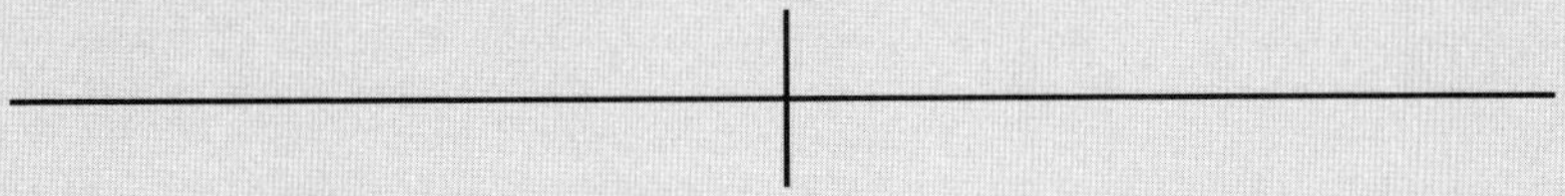

Write the **simple subject** before the vertical line and the *main verb* (predicate) after. The first word of the sentence must be capitalized, even in a diagram. No ending punctuation, commas, colons, quotation marks, or semicolons are used in a diagram.

Charlie *snores*!

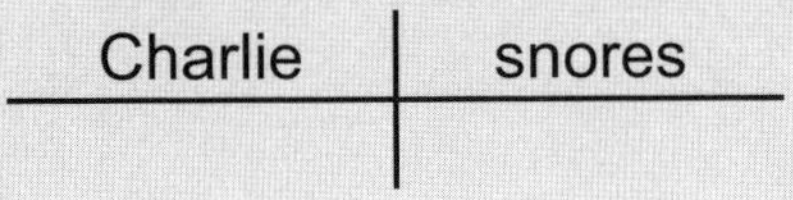

Charlie | snores

1. Each sentence diagram below has an error. Diagram each sentence correctly.

   a. Cats purr.

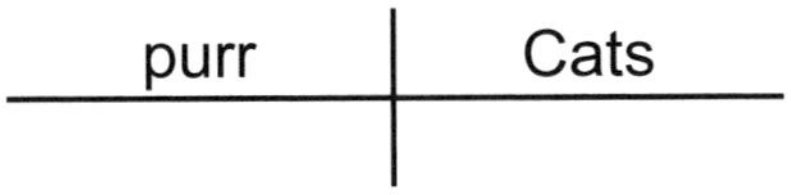

   purr | Cats

   b. Chickens cluck.

   Chickens | cluck

   c. Artists draw.

   Artists draw

Helping verbs are diagrammed with the *main verb* on the right side of the vertical subject/predicate line.

We will *sing*!

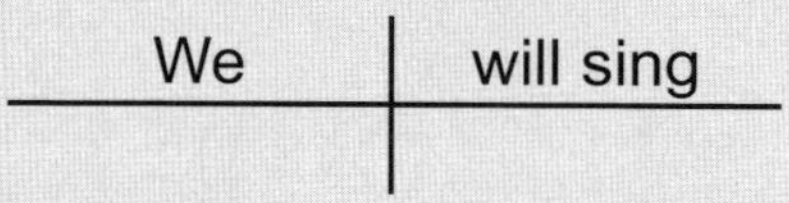

We	will sing

The **subject** of a sentence can be a noun or a pronoun.

Ben hiccupped.

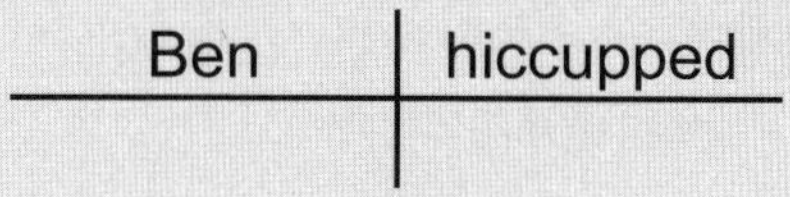

Ben	hiccupped

He hiccupped.

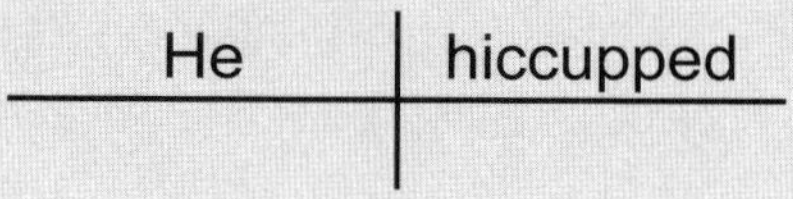

He	hiccupped

2. Fill in the diagram for each sentence.

a. Flowers grow.

b. Emily should read.

c. She sneezed.

d. They had eaten.

3. Write a sentence to match each diagram. Then complete the diagram.

a. ....

b. ....

c. ....

d. ....

If the subject is a **two-word name**, the whole name is diagrammed on the main line.

Uncle Fritz snores.

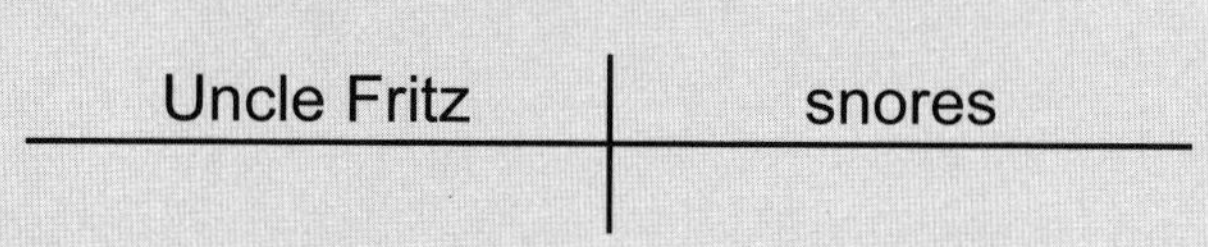

Uncle Fritz	snores

Mrs. Anderson might go.

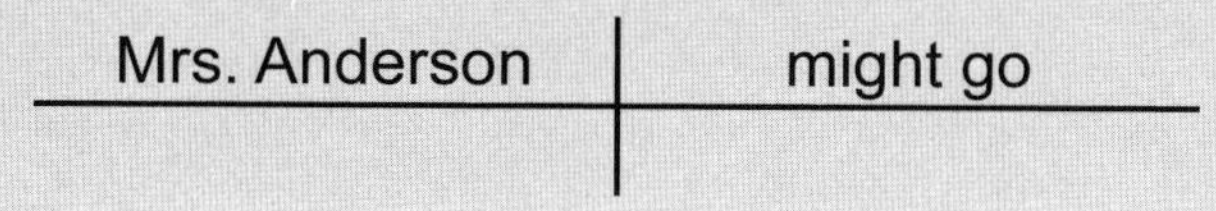

Mrs. Anderson	might go

4. Diagram each sentence.

 a. Mimi bakes.

 b. He has spoken.

 c. Mr. Cavanaugh tripped.

 d. Grandma Polly will visit.

Lesson 2: Direct Object

The **direct object** is a noun receiving the action of the *verb*. It answers "what?" after the verb.

Francis *eats* **cookies**.

What did Frances eat? Cookies, so cookies is the direct object.

Write the **direct object** on the main line after the vertical line separating the verb from the direct object.

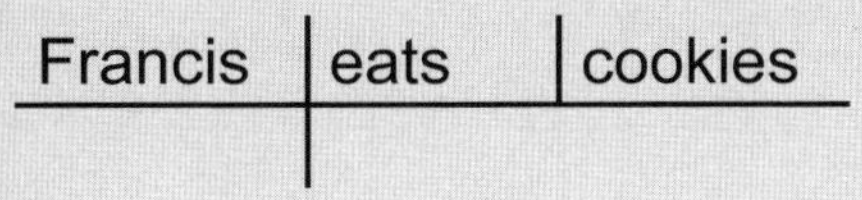

Francis	eats	cookies

1. Each sentence diagram below has an error. Diagram each sentence correctly.

a. Joey is playing cards.

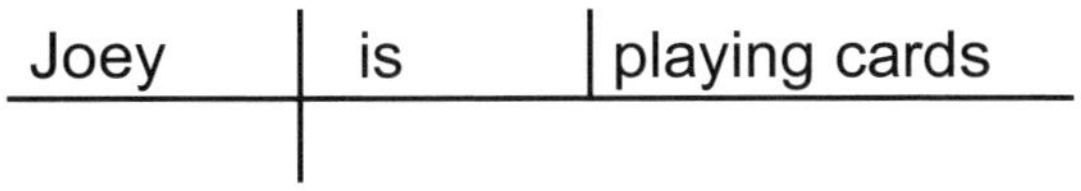

Joey	is	playing cards

b. We baked cupcakes.

We	baked	cupcakes

c. Uncle Mike has eaten squid.

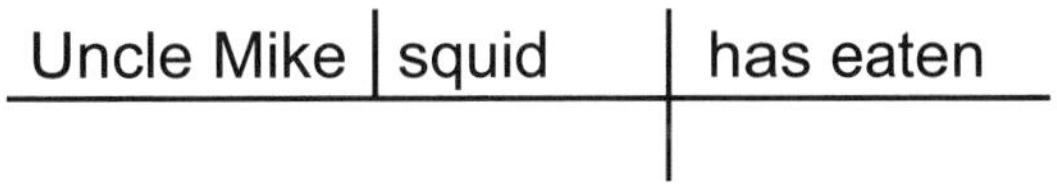

Uncle Mike	squid	has eaten

2. Fill in the diagram for each sentence.

a. Bees make honey.

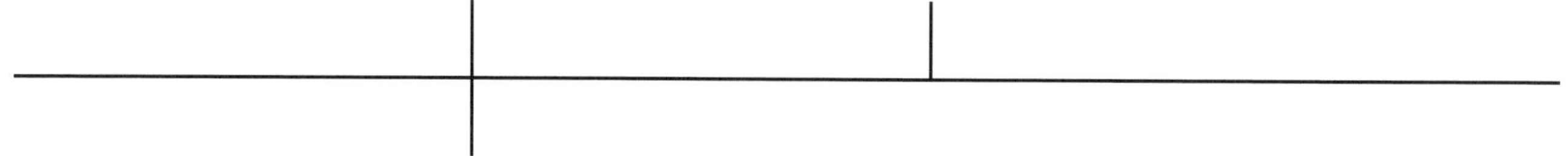

b. Uncle Fred builds cars.

c. Mrs. McDonald teaches preschool.

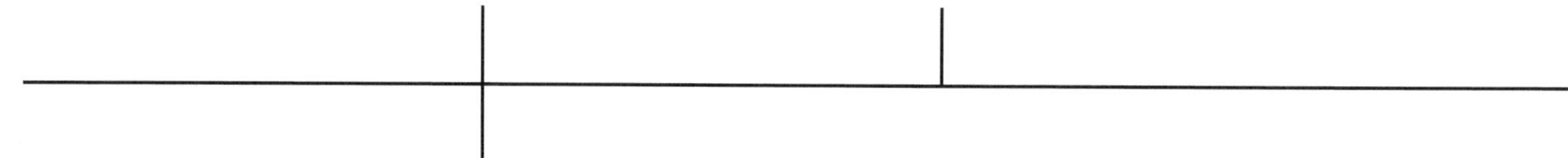

d. Principal Suarez wears suits.

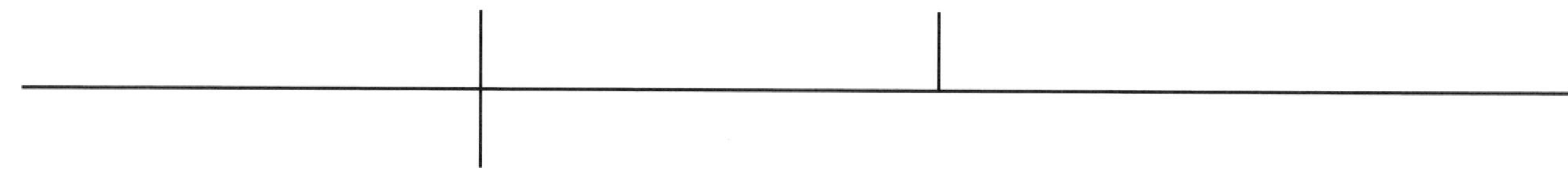

3. Write a sentence to match each diagram. Then complete the diagram.

a. ....

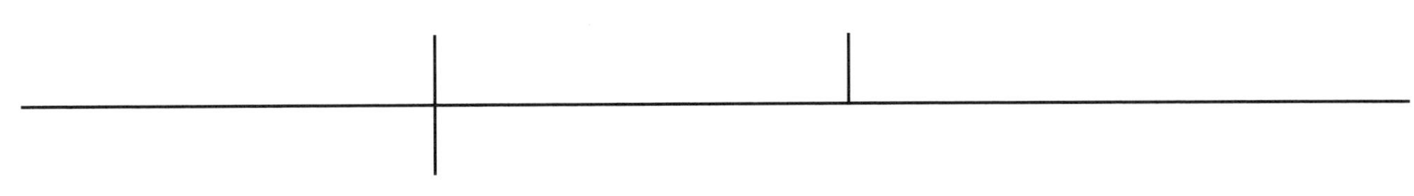

b. ....

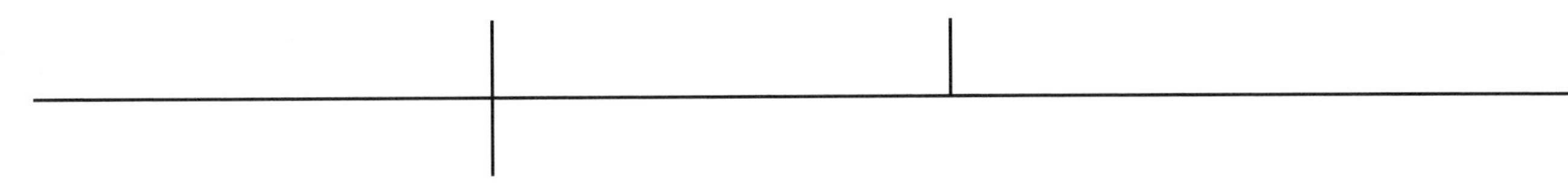

c. ....

d. ....

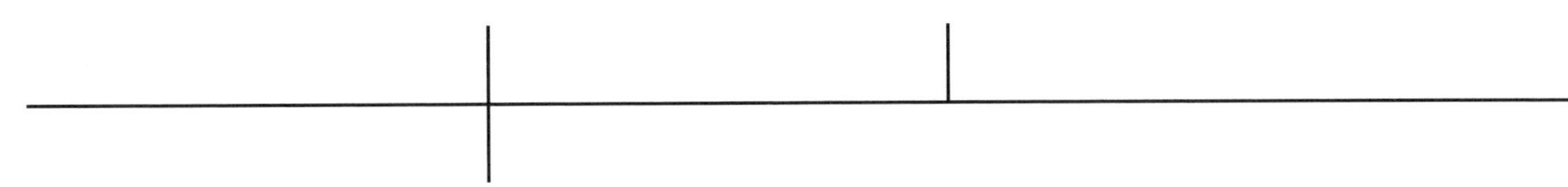

The title of a book, movie, poem, or song can also be the direct object. Any words that are capitalized in the sentence should be capitalized in the diagram.

Mr. Tandoori sang "**America**"!

Mr. Tandoori	sang	America

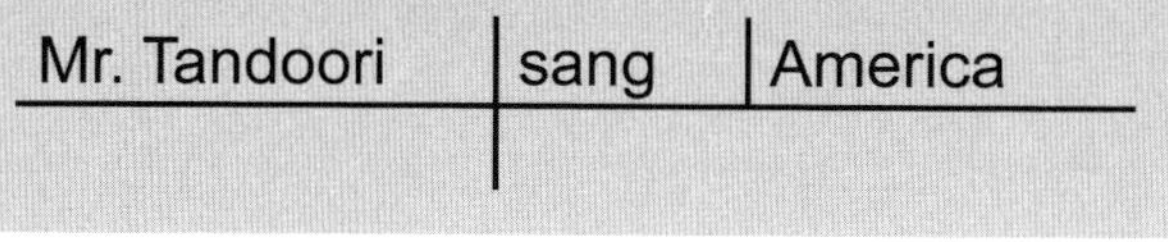

4. Diagram each sentence.

   a. Francis Scott Key wrote "The Star Spangled Banner."

   b. I read "Jabberwocky."

   c. They saw *The Avengers*.

   d. Aunt Cindy will watch *Cinderella*.

Lesson 3: Adjectives

An **adjective** modifying (describing) the subject or direct object is diagrammed on a slanted line below the noun it is modifying.

Ripe apples make **delicious** pie.

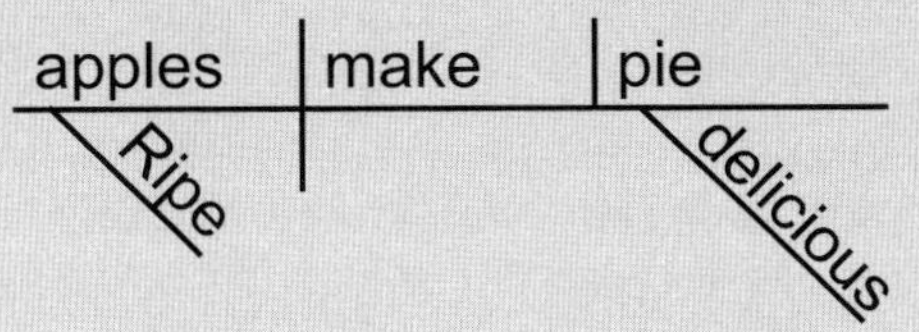

Old Uncle Herman eats **raw** eggs.

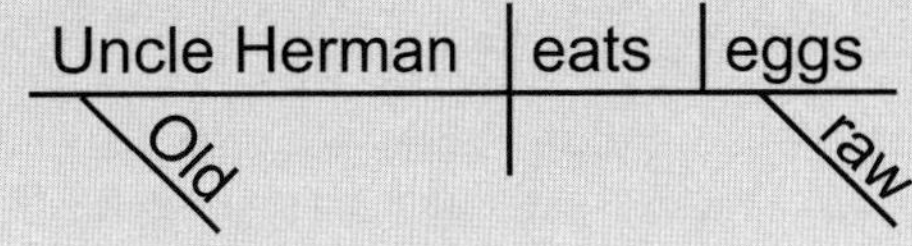

1. Each sentence diagram below has an error. Diagram each sentence correctly.

a. My dog chews dirty socks.

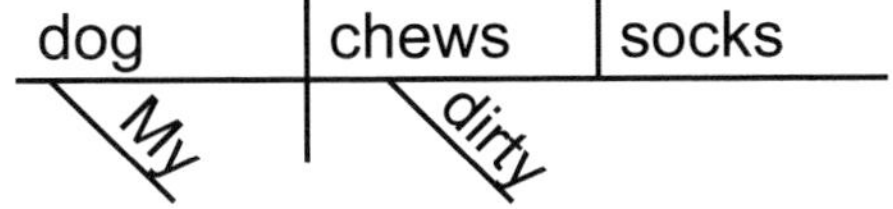

b. Mr. Scott carves scary pumpkins.

Mr. Scott | carves | pumpkins
scary

c. Huge bulldozers scooped the dirt.

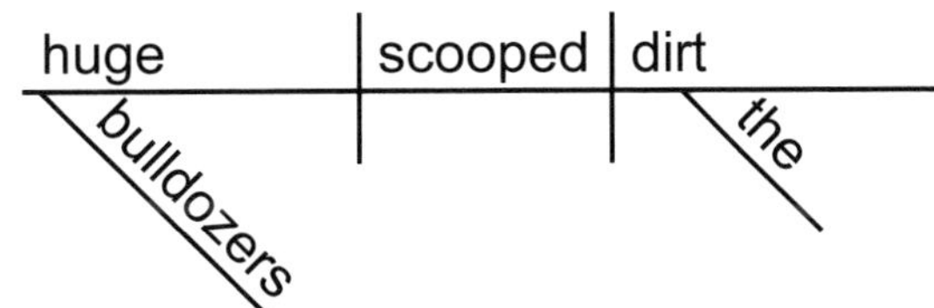

Numbers and possessive nouns act as **adjectives** and are diagrammed on a diagonal line below the noun.

Ms. Peters ate **three** cupcakes!

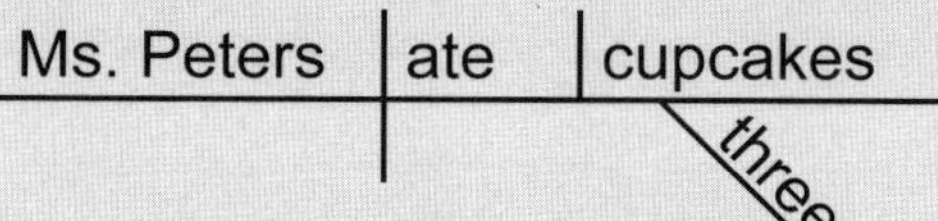

Stacey's cat eats tuna.

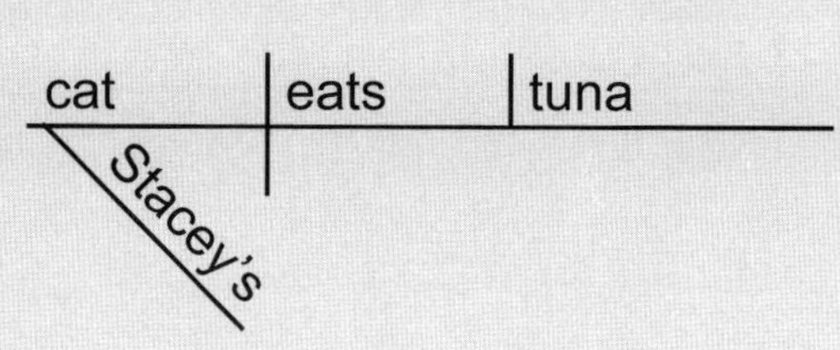

2. Fill in the diagram for each sentence.

a. My sisters chase squirrels.

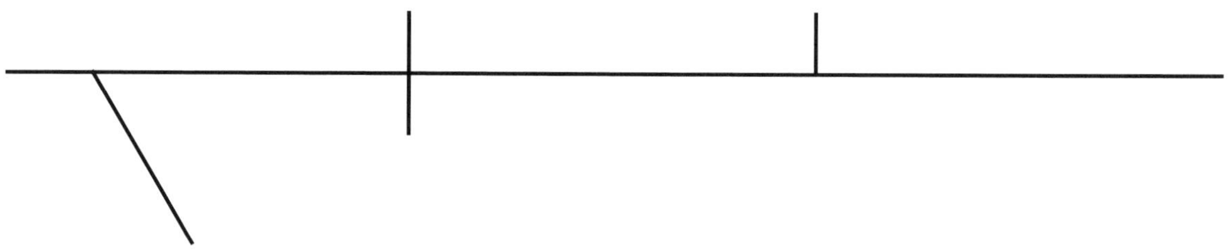

b. Julian ate eight meatballs.

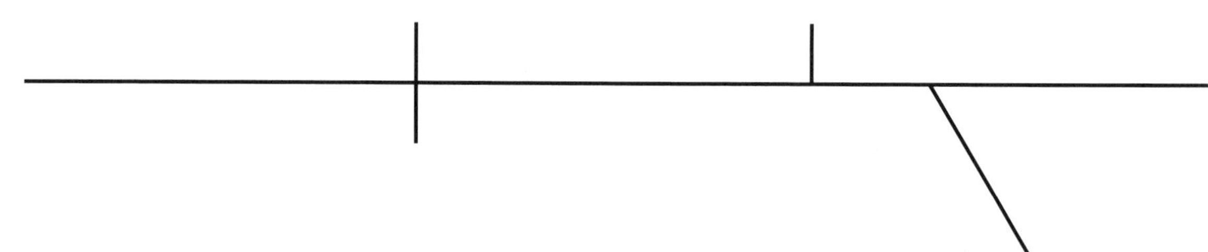

c. Fiona's friend can ride a unicycle.

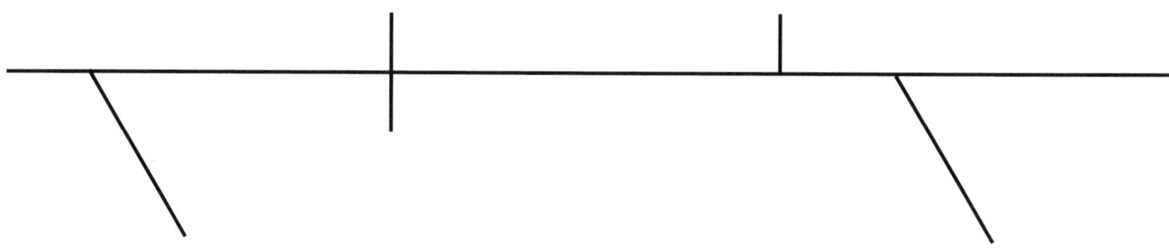

When two or more **adjectives** modify (describe) a noun, they all are diagrammed on diagonal lines below the noun. If they are joined by a coordinating conjunction, the conjunction is placed on a dotted line connecting the two adjectives.

Coordinating Conjunctions

and but or nor

Aleah bought **two colorful** umbrellas.

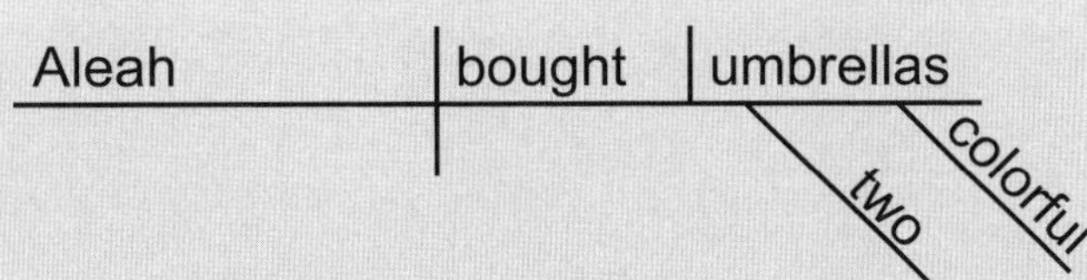

The black *and* **white** cat caught **a** mouse.

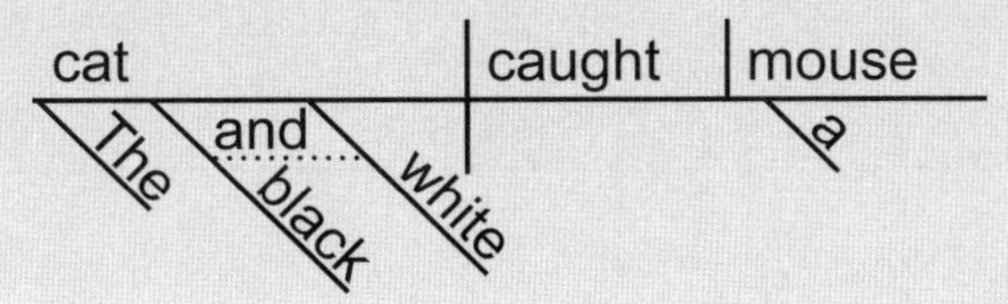

3. Write a sentence to match each diagram. Then complete the diagram.

a. ....

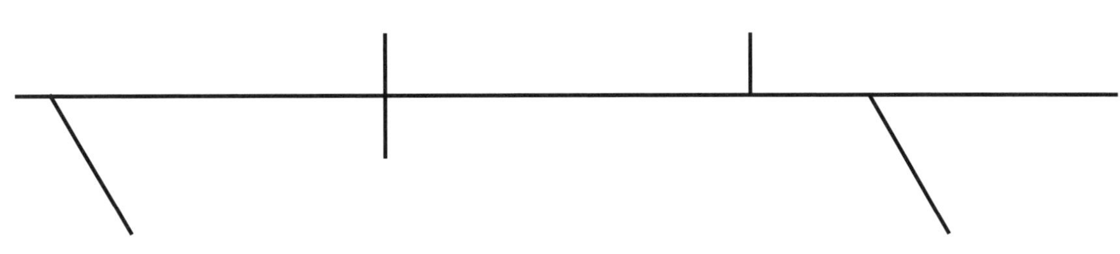

b. ....

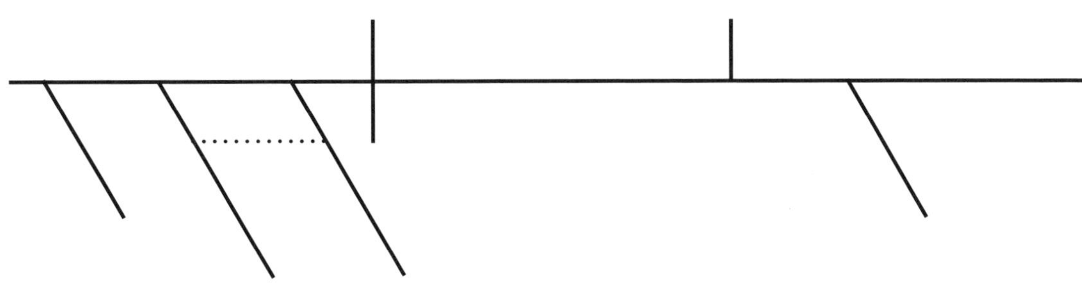

4. Diagram each sentence.

   a. Seven swans are swimming.

   b. Your hungry and smelly goat ate my new shoes!

   c. I bought a used but clean American flag.

   d. The mail carrier delivered five birthday cards.

Lesson 4: Adverbs Modifying Verbs

An **adverb** modifying (describing) the *verb* is diagrammed on a slanted line below the verb it is modifying. Adverbs tell when, where, or how the action is happening. They often end in "-ly".

My dog *barks* **loudly**.

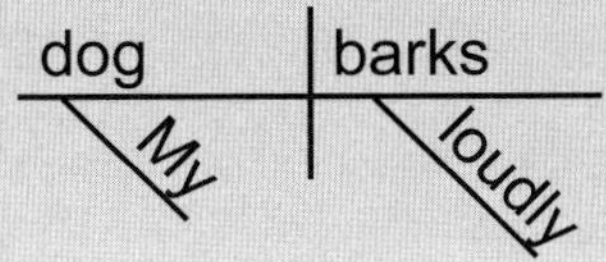

The horses *run* **fast!**

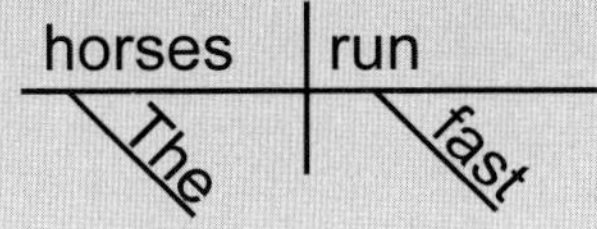

1. Each sentence diagram below has an error. Diagram each sentence correctly.

a. Mr. Sanchez sneezes often.

Mr. Sanchez | sneezes | often

b. My granny sews well.

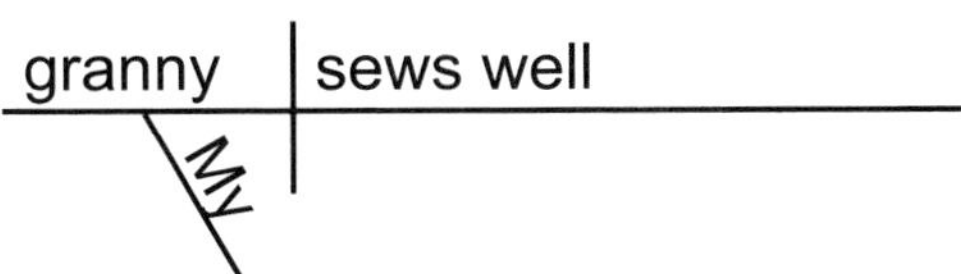

c. The tiny kittens mewed softly.

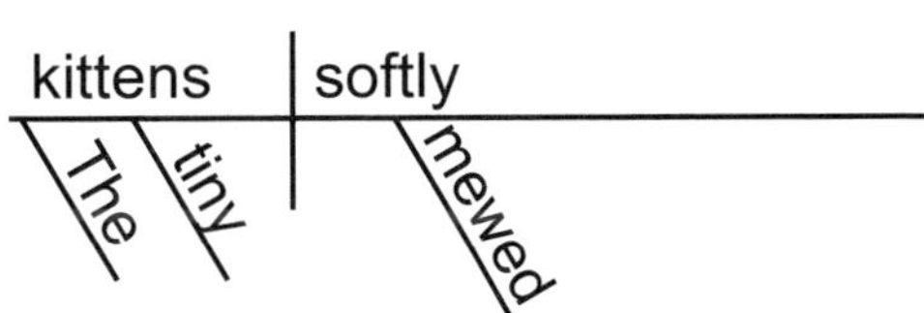

Adverbs can be placed anywhere in the sentence, not just next to the verb. They are always diagrammed on a diagonal line below the *verb*.

Sweetly, the birds *sang*.

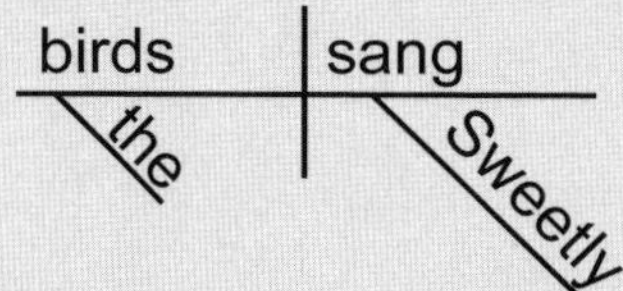

Two or more **adverbs** connected by a *conjunction* (and, or, but) that modify the same verb are diagrammed on diagonal lines below the verb. They are connected by a horizontal dotted line to diagram the conjunction.

Jimmy **quickly** *but* **carefully** built a snow fort.

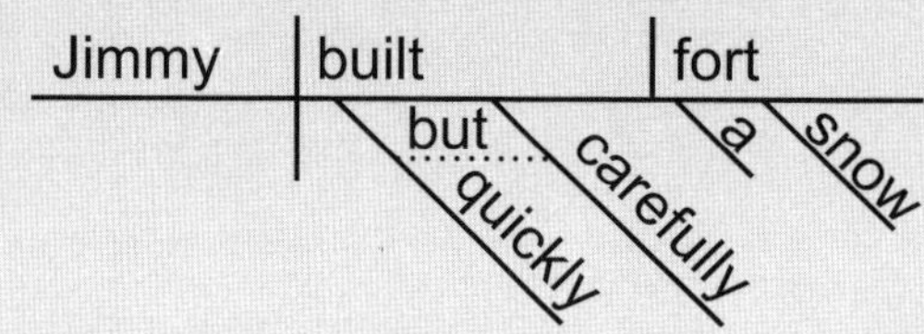

2. Fill in the diagram for each sentence.

a. Dad slurps soup loudly.

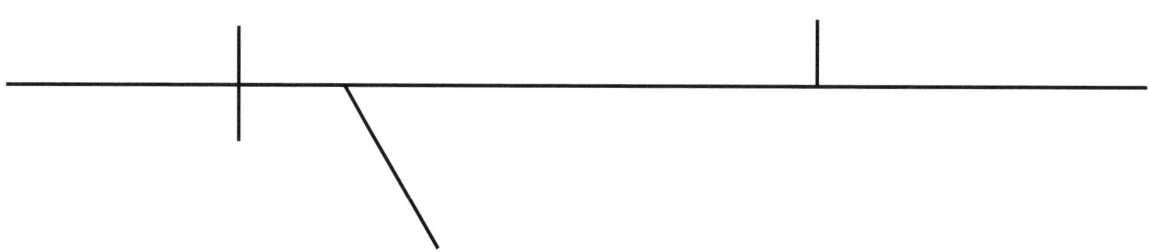

b. Three birds gracefully flew.

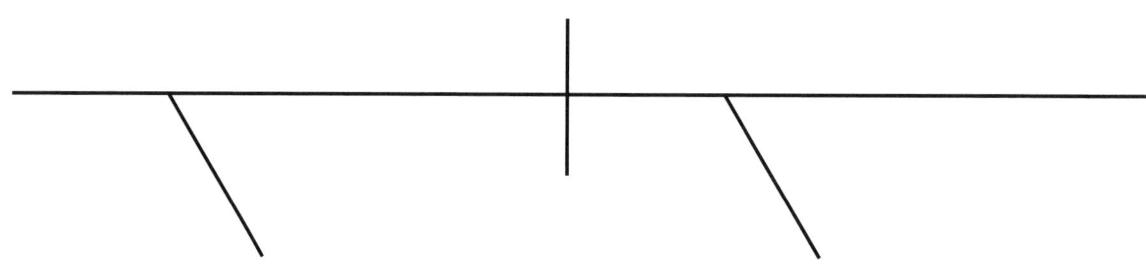

3. Write a sentence to match each diagram. Then complete the diagram.

a. ....

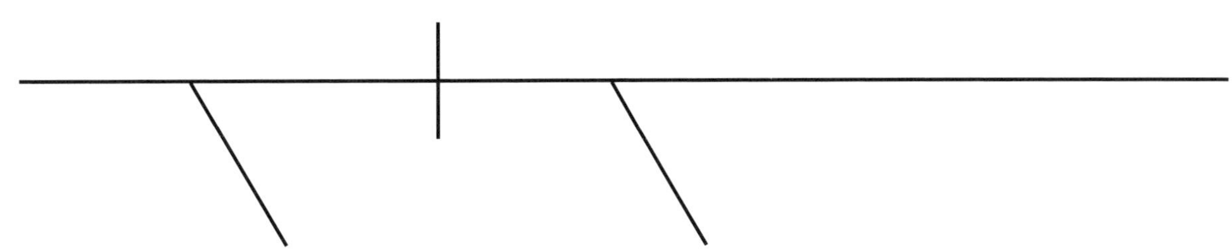

b. ....

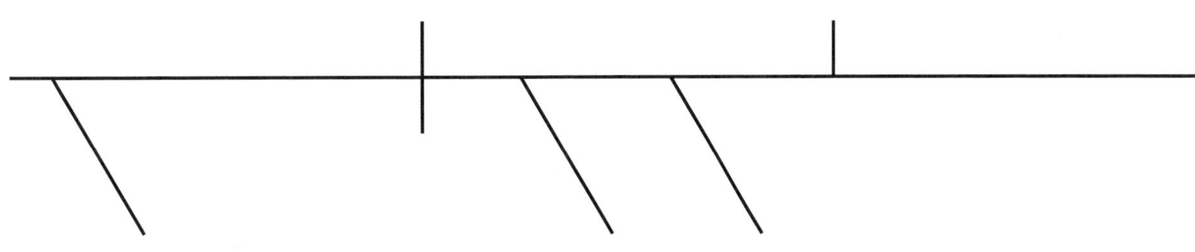

c. ....

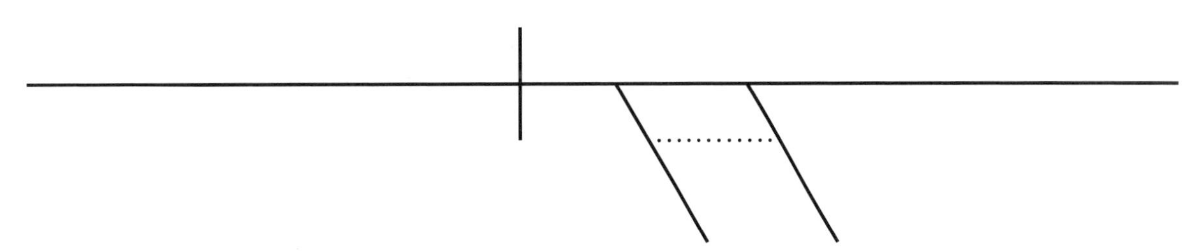

4. Diagram each sentence.

   a. Greedy Gus grinned gratefully.

   b. Quietly, Queen Quilla ate her quince.

   c. Seven sneaky spiders silently sucked blood.

   d. She sang loudly but sweetly.

Lesson 5: Predicate Adjectives

When a *linking verb* (is, am, are, was, were) is followed by an adjective which is modifying (describing) the <u>subject</u>, it is called a **predicate adjective**. It is diagrammed on the main line after the verb, separated by a slanted line.

<u>Cupcakes</u> *are* **delicious**.

Cupcakes | are \ delicious

The <u>elephant</u> *was* **gigantic**.

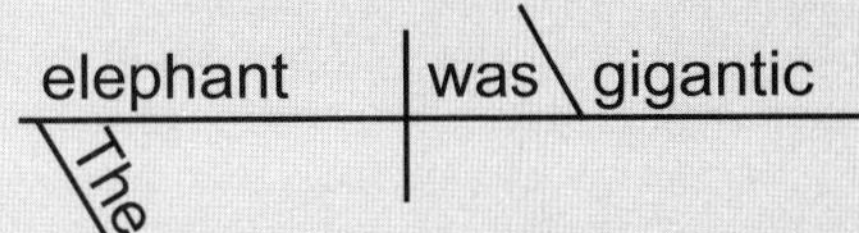

The **predicate adjective** can be a proper adjective. It should be capitalized.

Kai is **Hawaiian**.

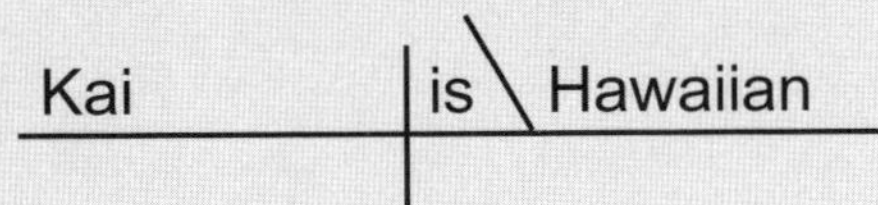

1. Each sentence diagram below has an error. Diagram each sentence correctly.

   a. The bicycles are rusty.

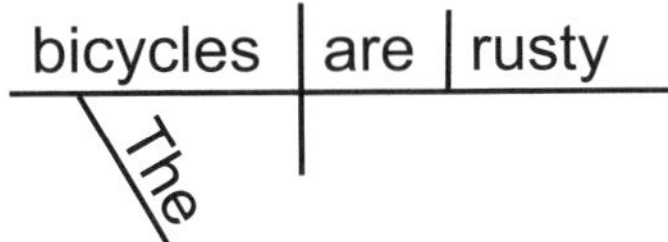

   b. Li Wei is Chinese.

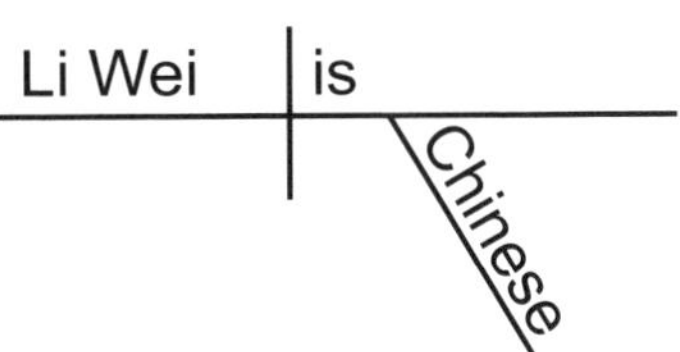

Adjectives that modify the subject and come before the *verb* are diagrammed below the subject. Adjectives that modify the subject noun and come after the *verb* are diagrammed on the main line after a slanted line.

Henry's **hot** cocoa *is* **horrible**.

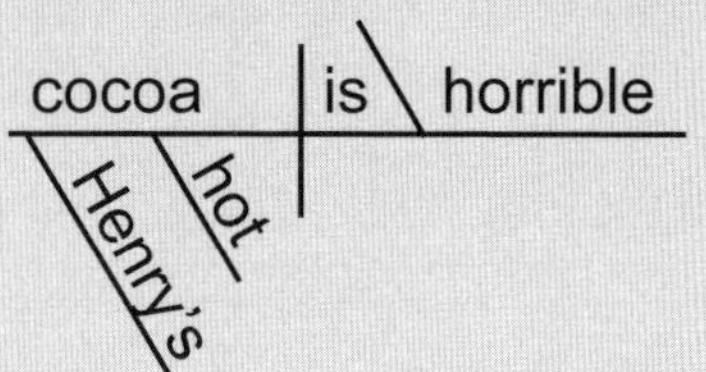

Ciaran's **crazy Christmas** cookies *are* **crunchy**!

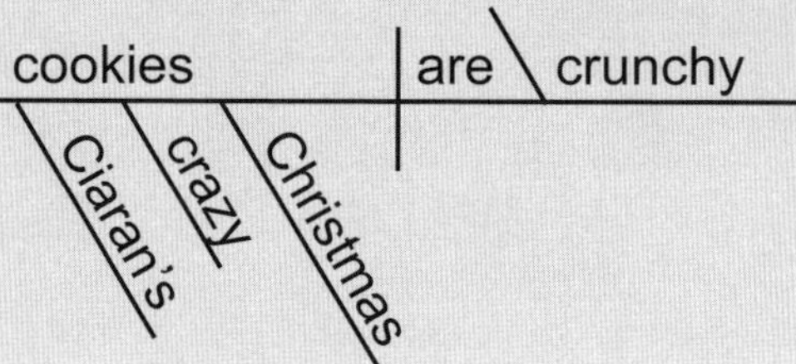

2. Fill in the diagram for each sentence.

   a. Sally was happy.

   b. Happy Harold is handsome.

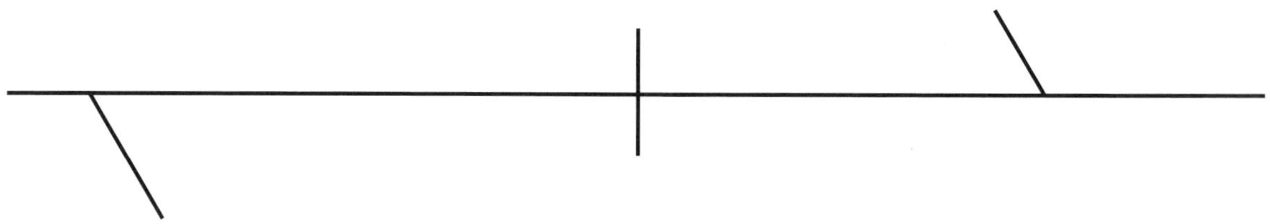

   c. Five flying flamingos are fancy.

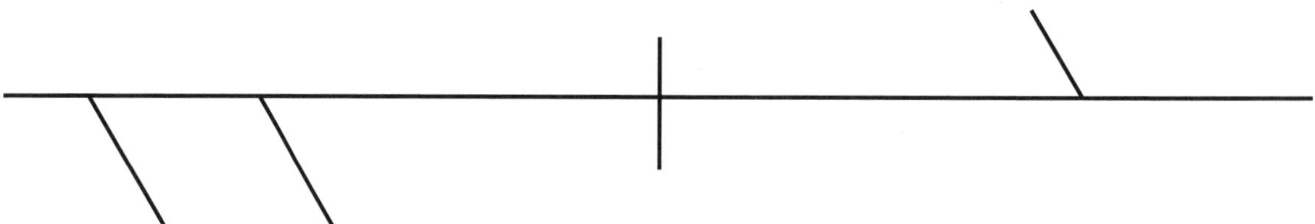

3. Write a sentence to match each diagram. Then complete the diagram.

a. ....

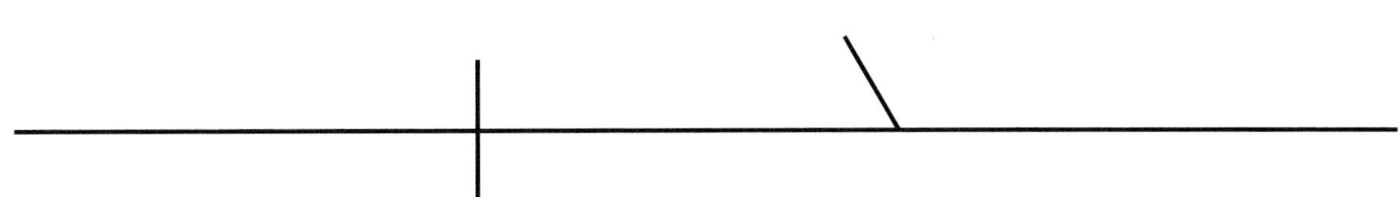

b. ....

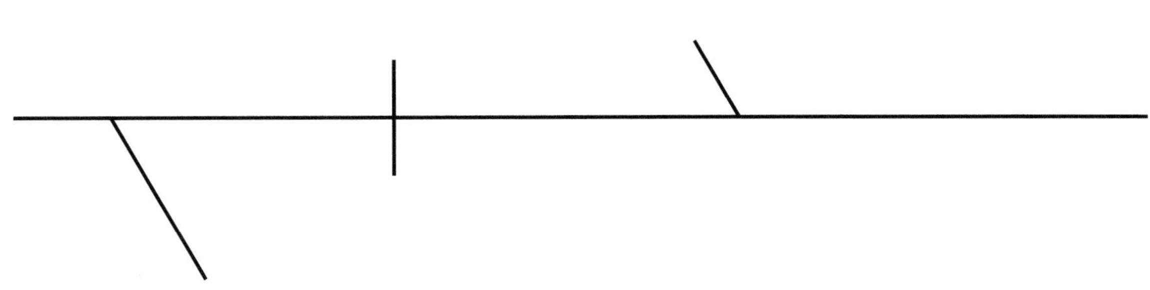

c. ....

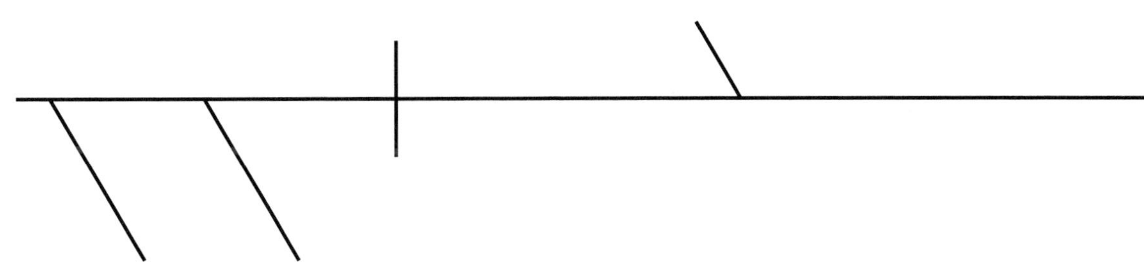

4. Diagram each sentence.

   a. Their flags are American.

   b. My three sons are silly.

   c. Her ten cats are cute.

   d. Papa's hamburgers are heavenly.

Lesson 6: Predicate Nouns

When a *linking verb* (is, am, are, was, were) is followed by a noun, it is called a **predicate noun**. It is diagrammed after the verb, separated by a slanted line.

Mr. Duffy *is* a **baker**.

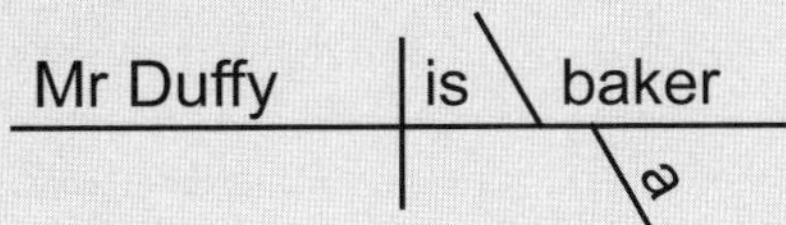

Any adjectives describing the **predicate noun** are diagrammed on a line below that noun.

Luciano Pavarotti *was* a great **tenor**.

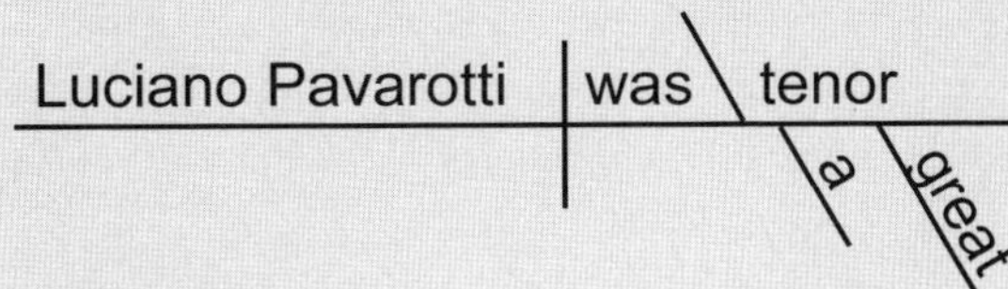

The **predicate noun** can be a proper noun or a pronoun. A proper noun should be capitalized.

My doctor is **Dr. Whitestone**.

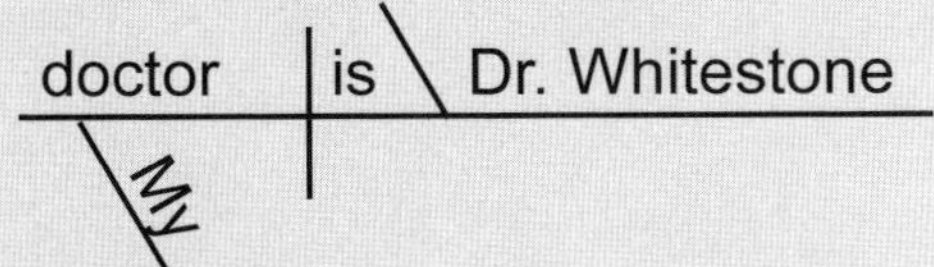

My older brother is **he**.

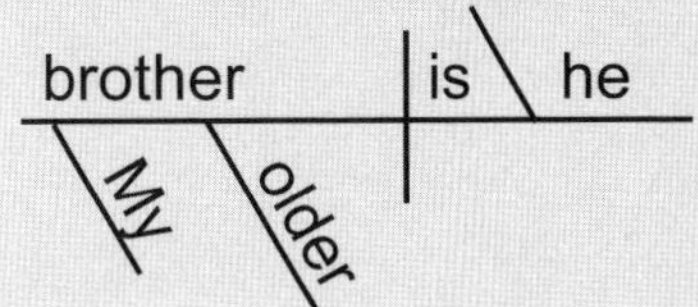

1. Each sentence diagram below has an error. Diagram each sentence correctly.

a. Mrs. Austin is a teacher.

Mrs. Austin | is \ teacher | a

b. I am a teenager.

I | am \ a | teenager

2. Fill in the diagram for each sentence.

a. They are our neighbors.

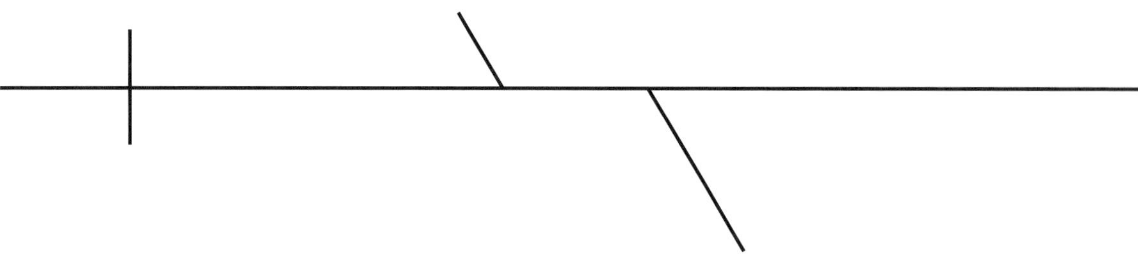

b. Talisa is my best friend.

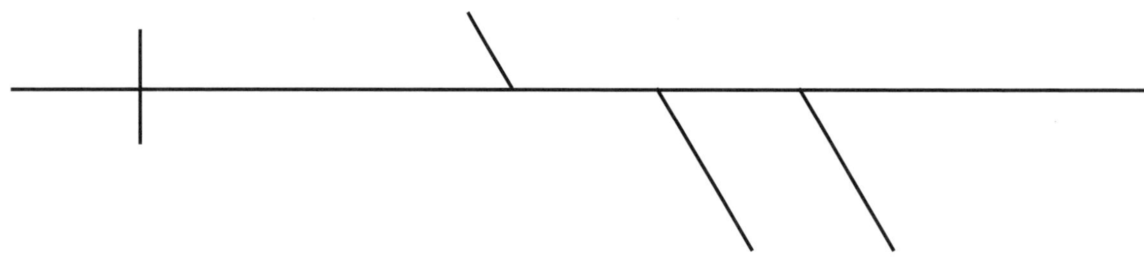

c. My favorite sport is soccer.

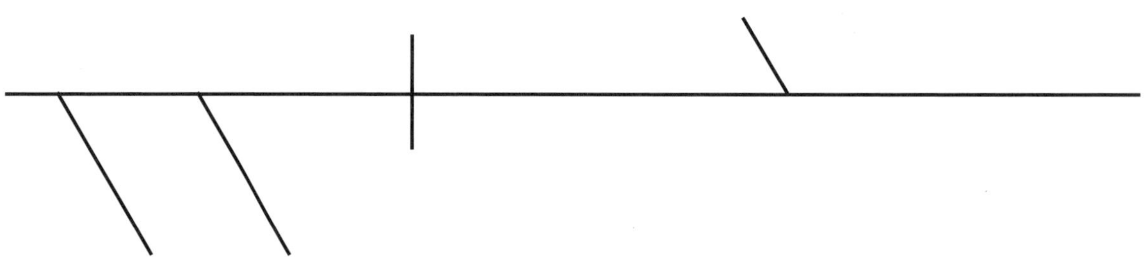

3. Write a sentence to match each diagram. Then complete the diagram.

a. ....

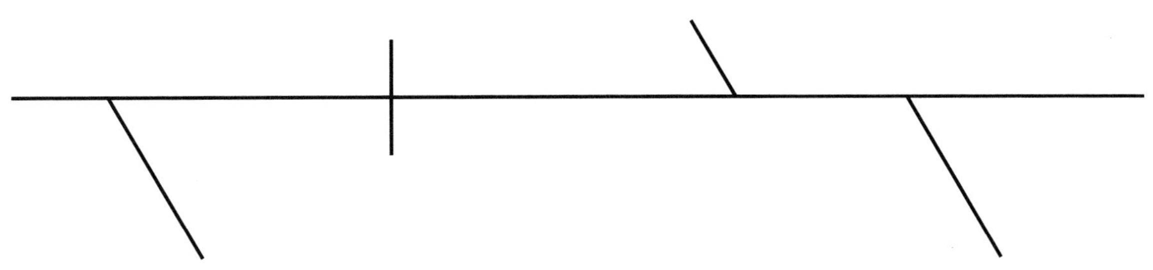

b. ....

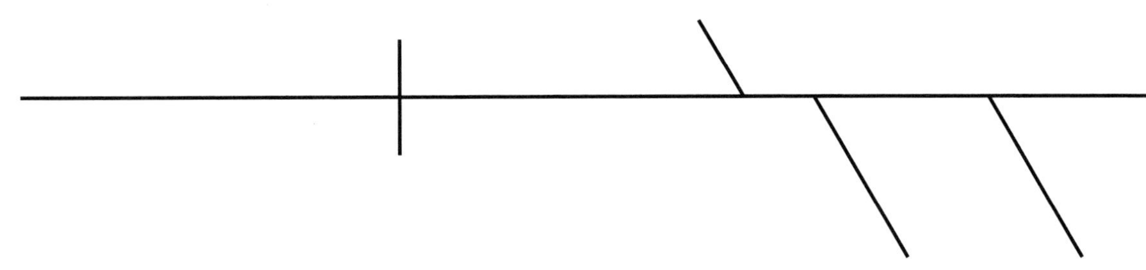

c. ....

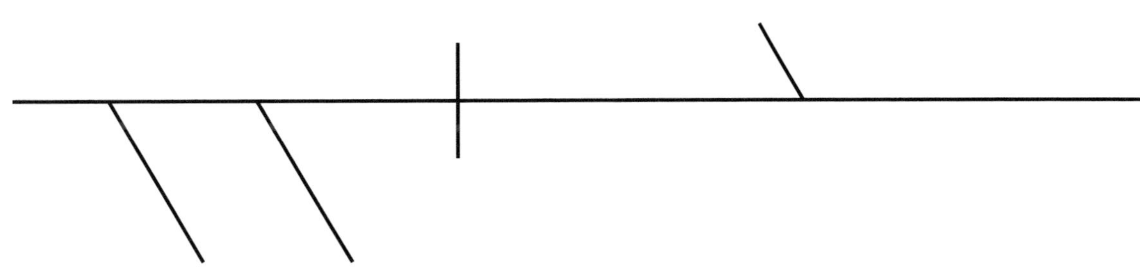

4. Diagram each sentence.

a. Lunch is ham sandwiches.

b. The sugar cookies are your gift.

c. Our first scout leader was she.

d. The two crazy kittens were best friends.

Lesson 7: Prepositional Phrases (Adjectival)

Prepositional phrases are groups of words beginning with a preposition and ending with a *noun*, known as the object of the preposition. They are often used to help modify (describe) the subject of the sentence.

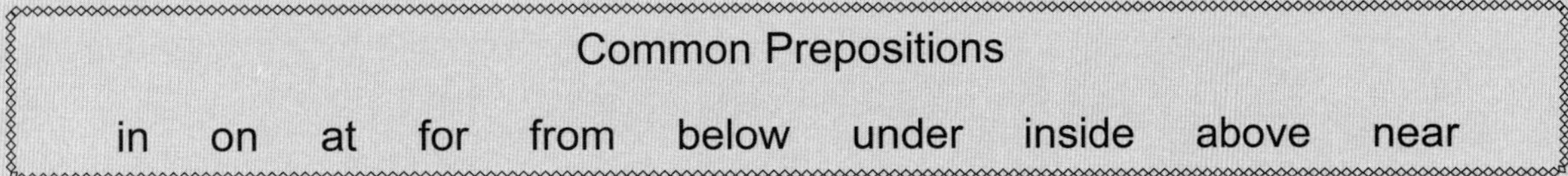

Prepositional phrases are diagrammed below the subject.

The ball **in the *yard*** is flat.

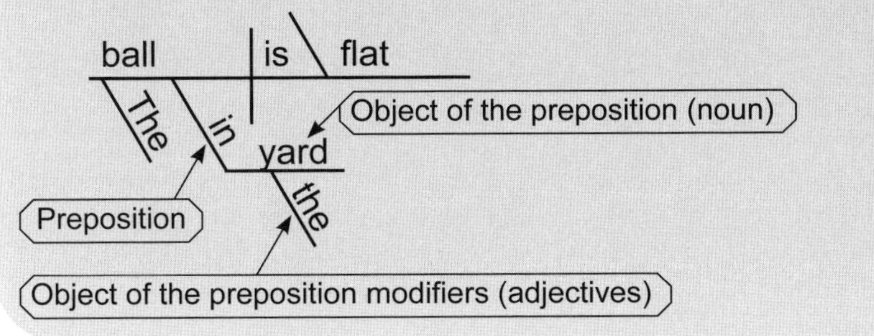

The boy **from *school*** ate some ice cream.

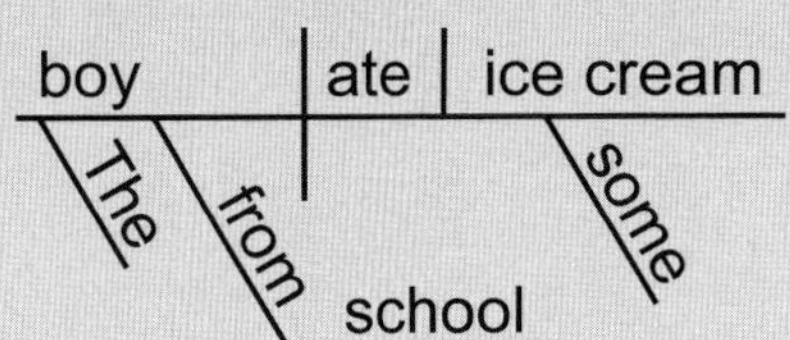

1. Each sentence diagram below has an error. Diagram each sentence correctly.

   a. The car in the garage needs gas.

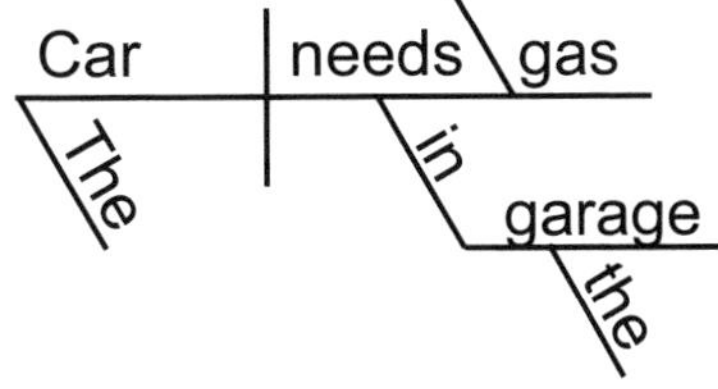

   b. The piano in the corner is old.

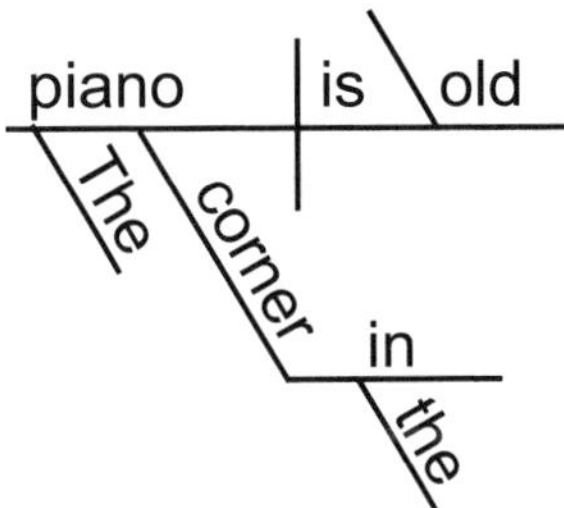

2. Fill in the diagram for each sentence.

a. The box under the table is yours.

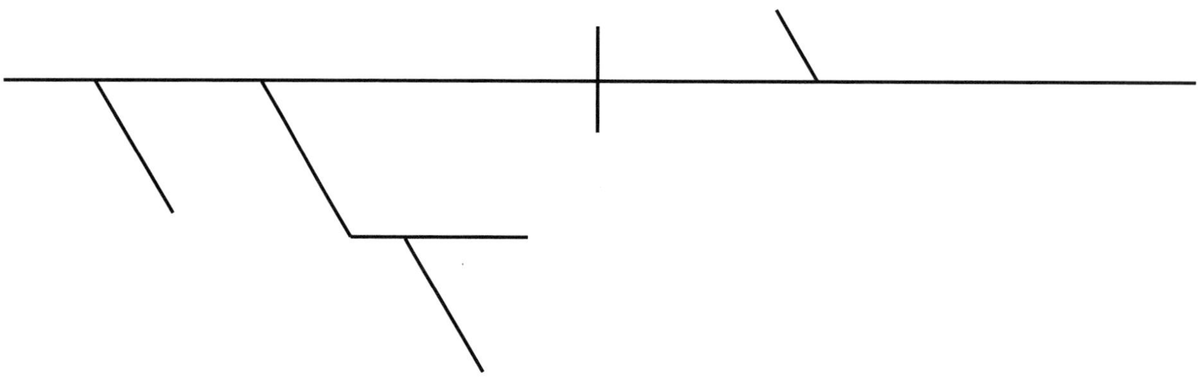

b. Your gift for Grandma is lovely!

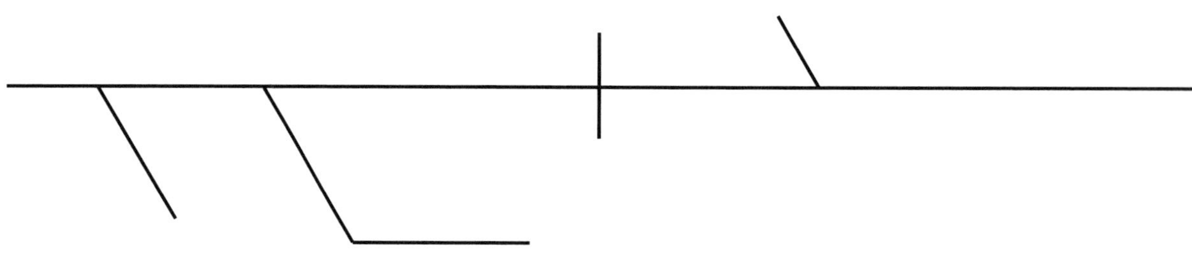

c. The gecko in my room eats crickets.

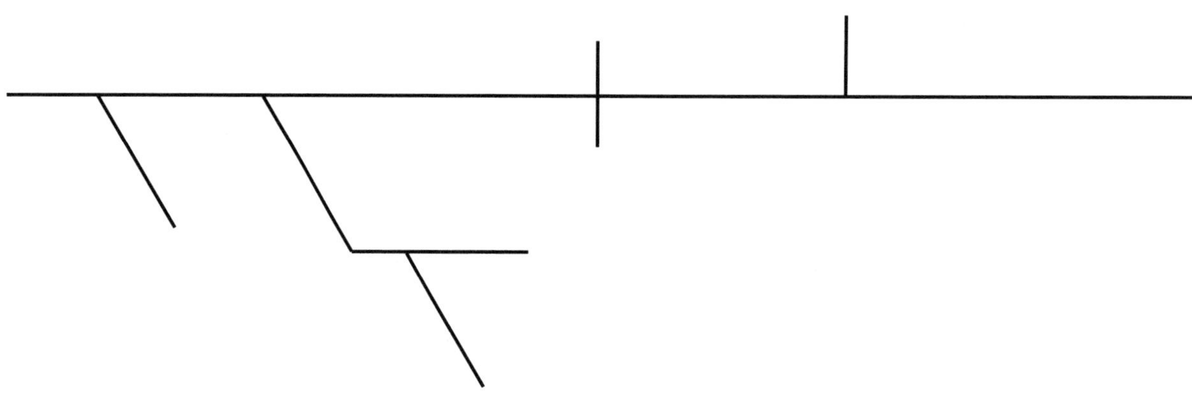

3. Write a sentence to match each diagram. Then complete the diagram.

a. ....

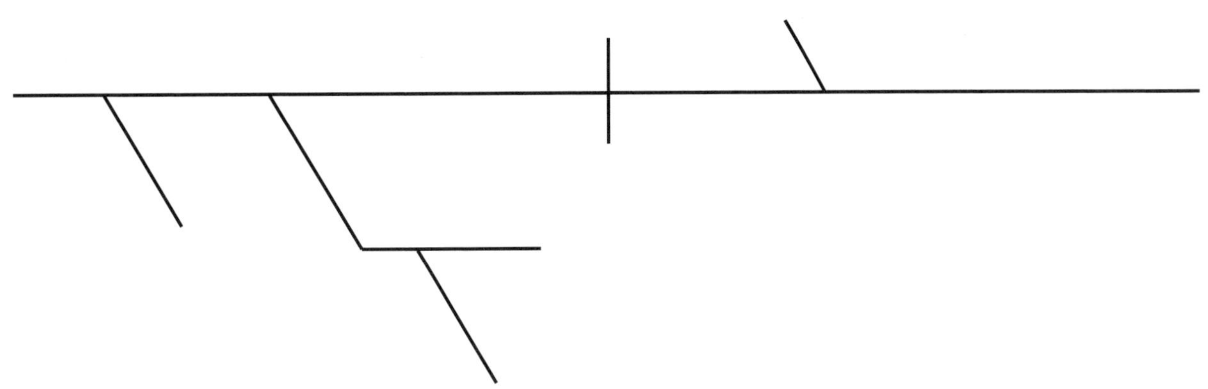

b. ....

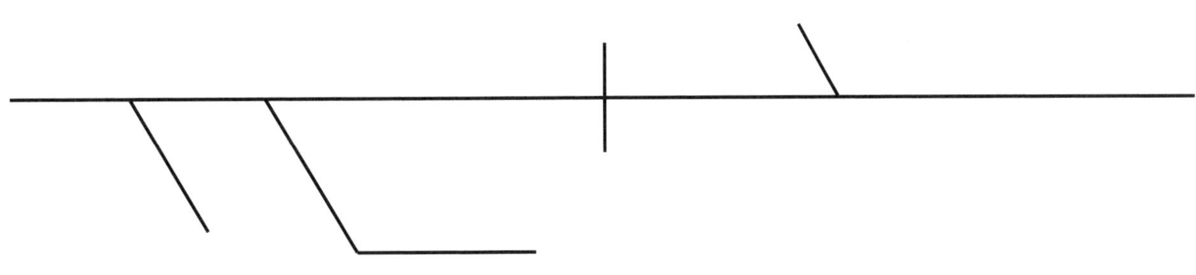

c. ....

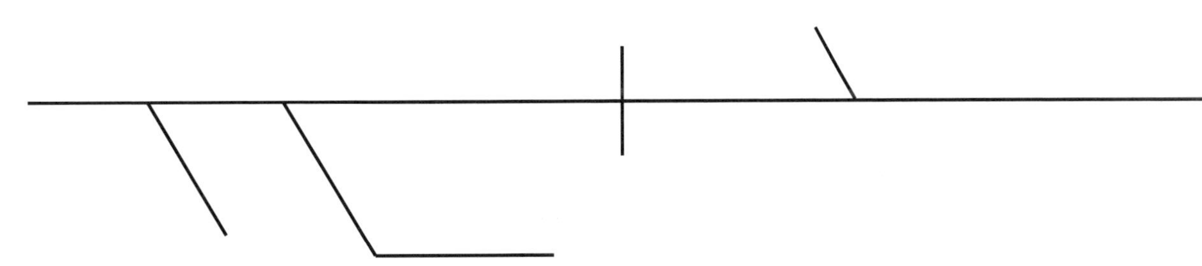

Prepositional phrases can also modify (describe) nouns in the predicate of the sentence, such as the direct object or predicate noun. They are diagrammed below the noun they modify.

Miranda decorated the <u>cookies</u> **at my house**.

Miranda | decorated | cookies
the
at
house
my

I love my <u>balloon</u> **from Red Robin**.

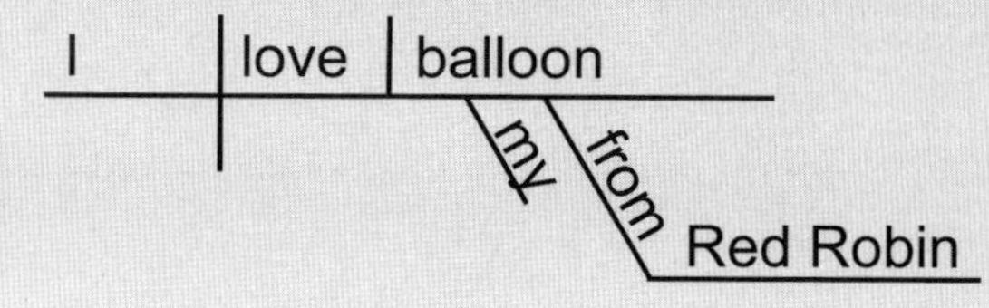

4. Diagram each sentence.

   a. The vase on the shelf is an antique.

   b. Our day at the beach was fun!

   c. Jeanne opened a letter from Lucy.

   d. I like the candy in the box.

Lesson 8: Prepositional Phrases (Adverbial)

Prepositional phrases can modify (describe) a *verb*, telling when or where that action happened. They are diagrammed below the verb.

She *jogged* **after school**.

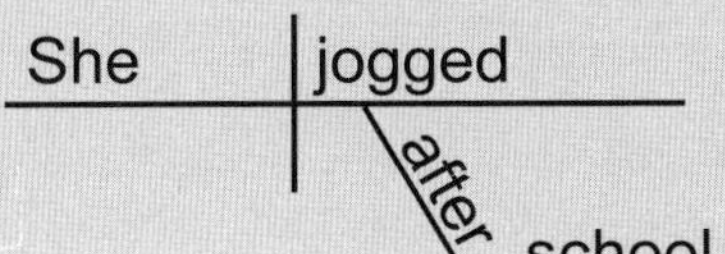

Aunt Anita *ate* apples **in the orchard**.

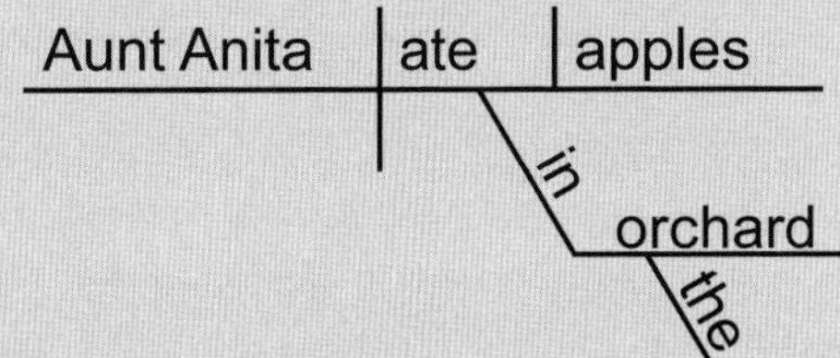

Common "When" Prepositions	Common "Where" Prepositions
before during after in (in three hours) at (at midnight)	beside under to near on over in (in the orchard) at (at her house)

1. Each sentence diagram below has an error. Diagram each sentence correctly.

   a. The bunny hopped over the fence.

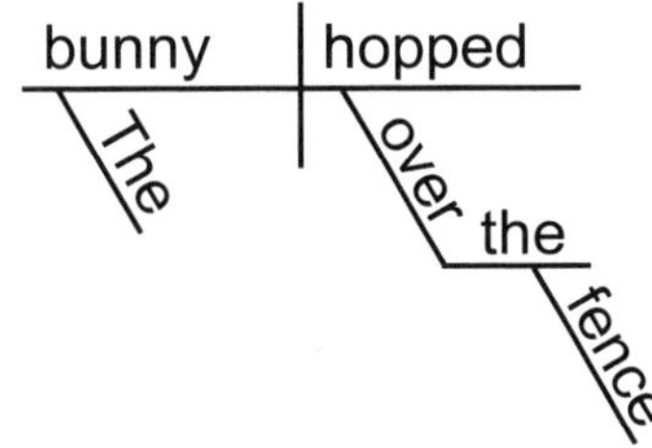

   b. Mom put the turkey in the oven.

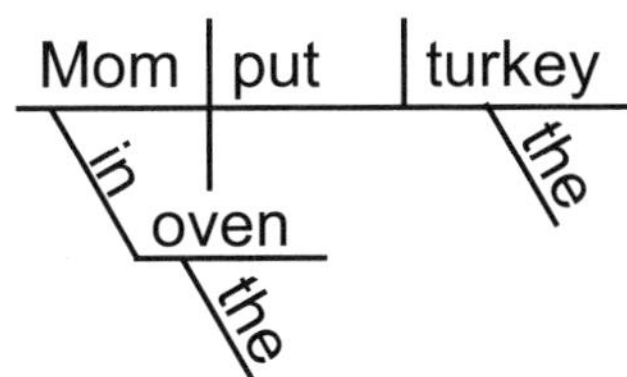

2. Fill in the diagram for each sentence.

a. The car rolled down the street.

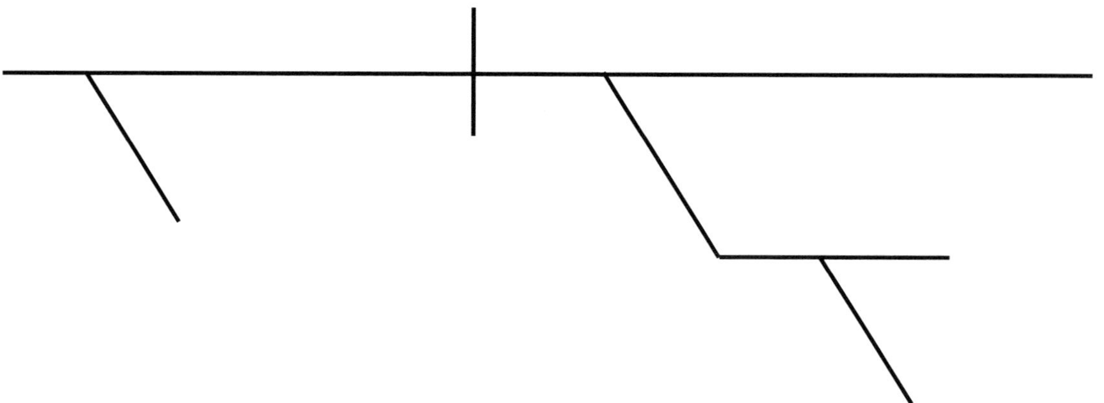

b. We played games after dinner.

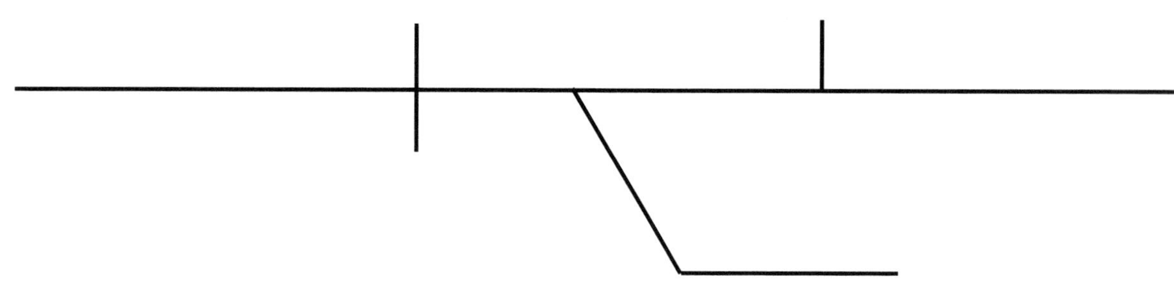

c. He is grumpy in the morning.

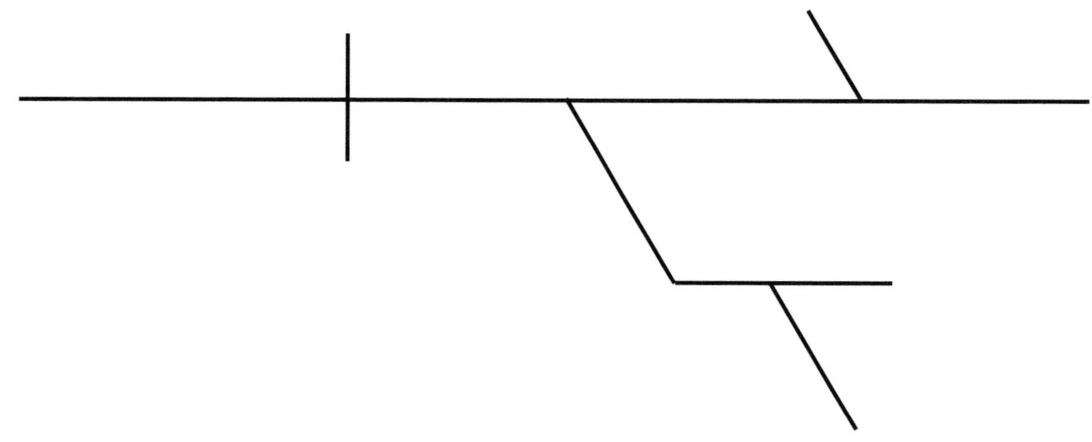

More than one **prepositional phrase** can modify (describe) a *verb* at the same time without a conjunction (and, but,or, nor). Often, one phrase will tell when something happened, and the other phrase tells *where*. They both are diagrammed below the verb.

Aunt Anita *ate* apples ***in the orchard*** **after dinner**.

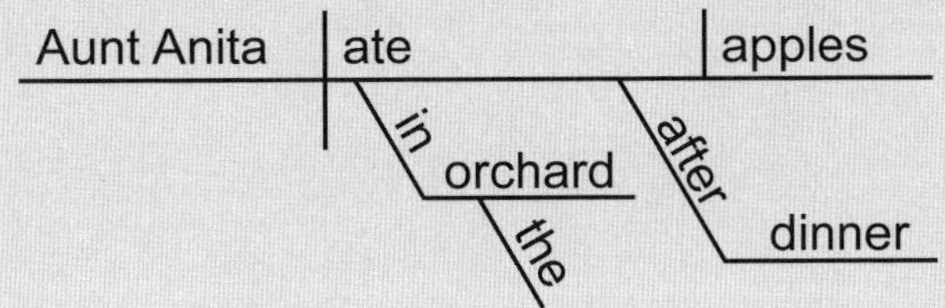

3. Write a sentence to match each diagram. Then complete the diagram.

a. ....

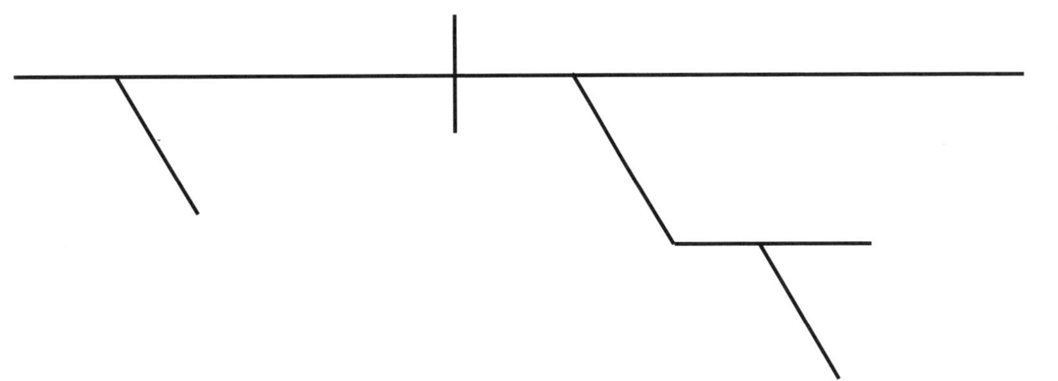

b. ....

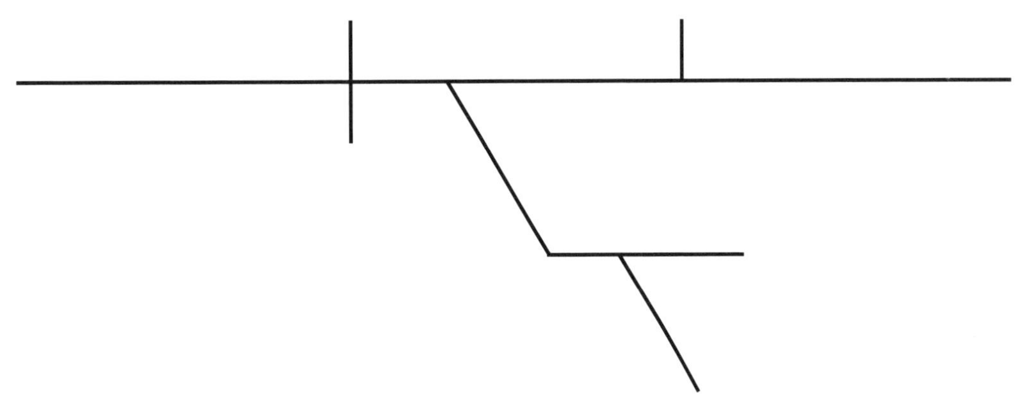

c. ....

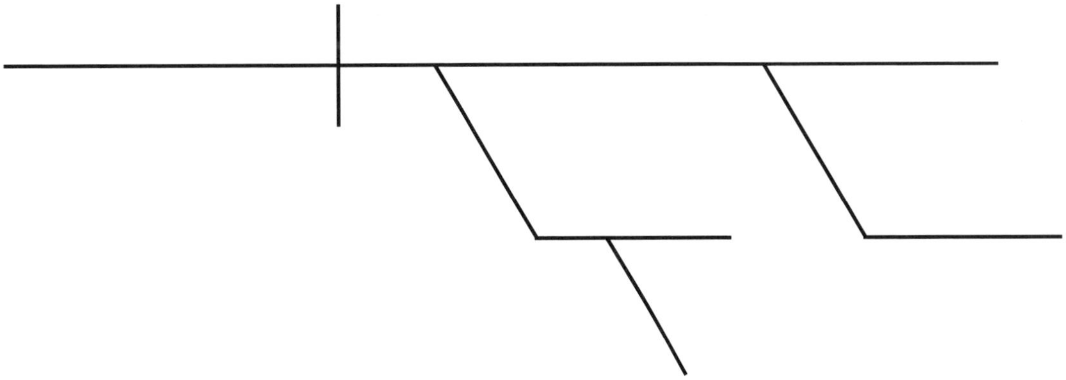

4. Diagram each sentence.

   a. The flag fluttered in the breeze.

   b. They will sing "Happy Birthday" before dessert.

   c. I will see the movie at the theater on Tuesday.

   d. Patrick reads books in his room at night.

Lesson 9: Compound Subjects

Compound subjects (two or more nouns or pronouns) are diagrammed in order, one above the other, with the *coordinating conjunction* joining them together on a dotted vertical line.

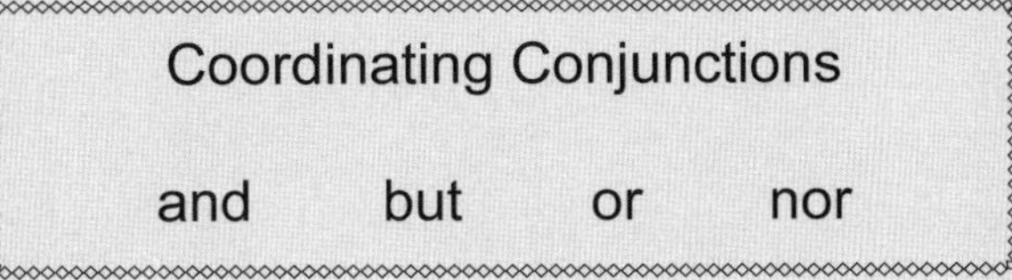

Wyatt *and* **Laryssa** are best friends.

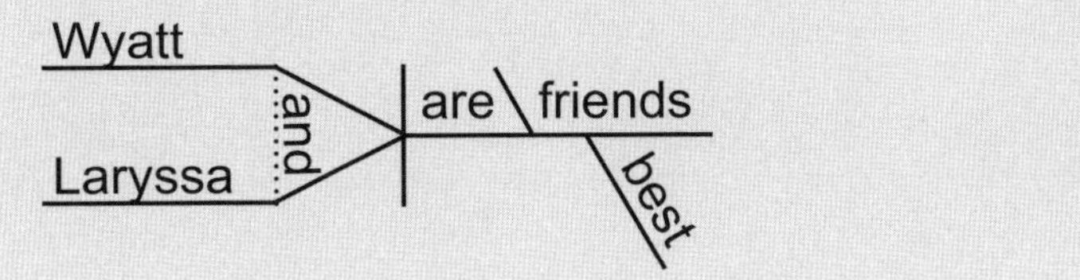

Jonah, **Sarah**, *or* **Meriah** ate my hamburger!

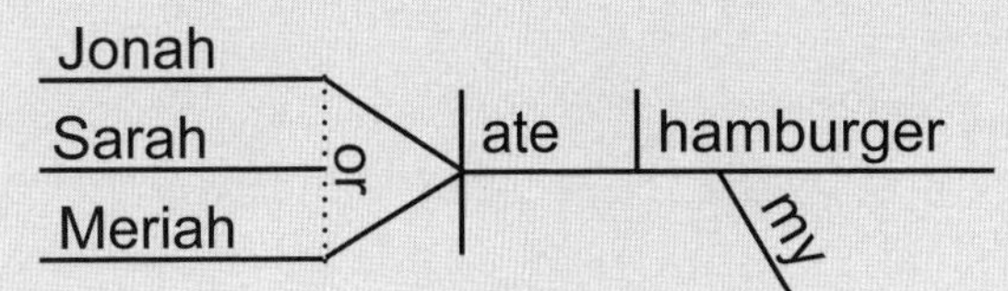

1. Each sentence diagram below has an error. Diagram each sentence correctly.

   a. Mom or Dad will call you.

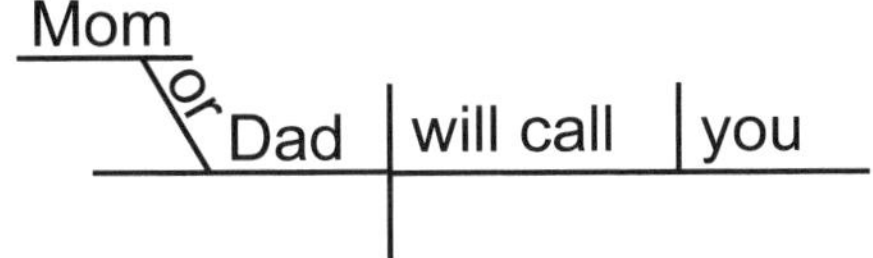

   b. Curtis and Caylee are twins.

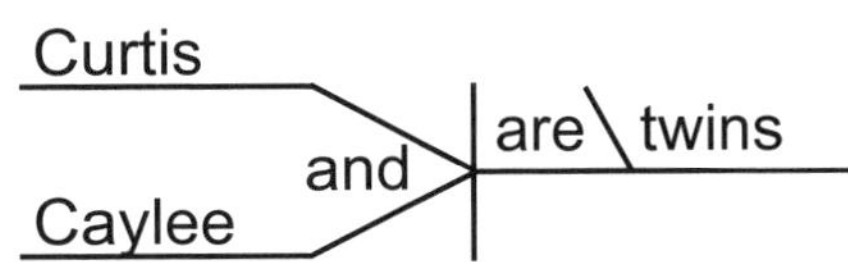

2. Fill in the diagram for each sentence.

   a. Cinderella and Snow White sing beautifully.

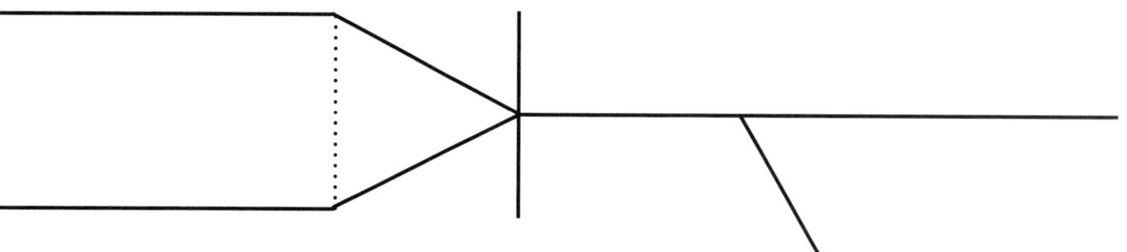

   b. Grace or Elias ate the bagels.

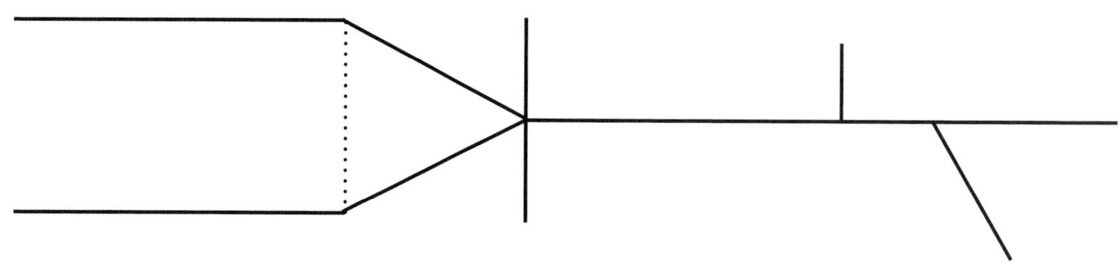

   c. Jimmy and Joey watch movies in the basement.

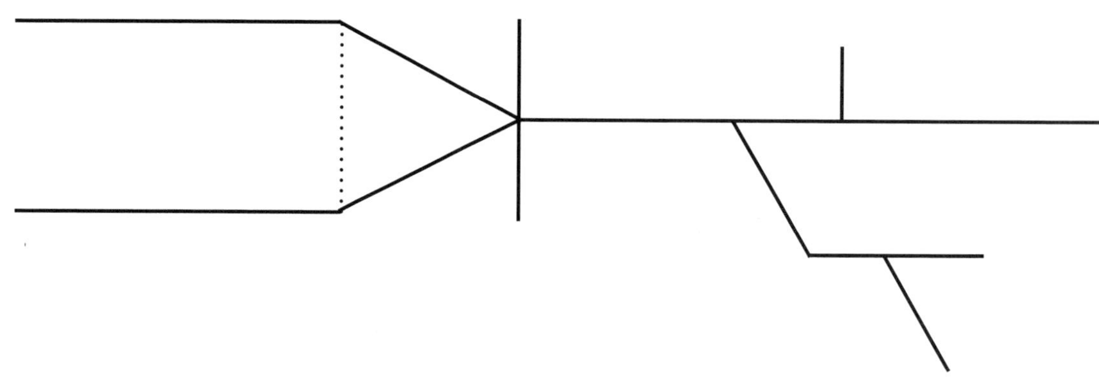

3. Write a sentence to match each diagram. Then complete the diagram.

a. ....

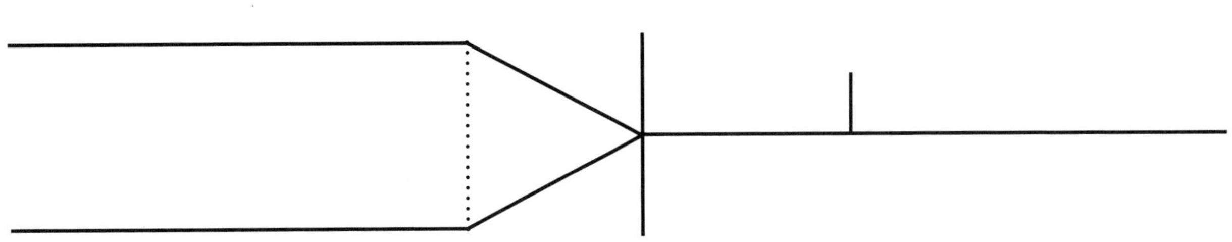

b. ....

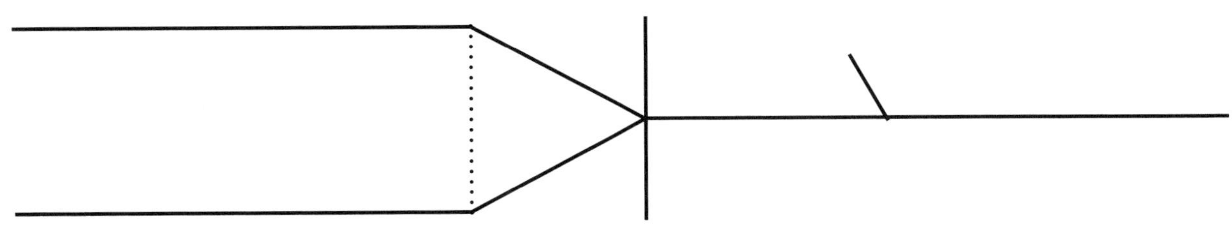

c. ....

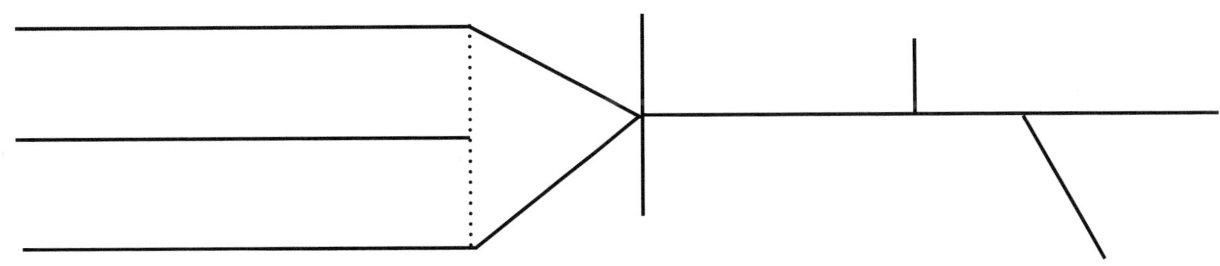

Any *adjectives* that modify (describe) the **compound subjects** are diagrammed on the line below the noun they are modifying.

The old **dog** and *the young* ***cat*** are *best* friends.

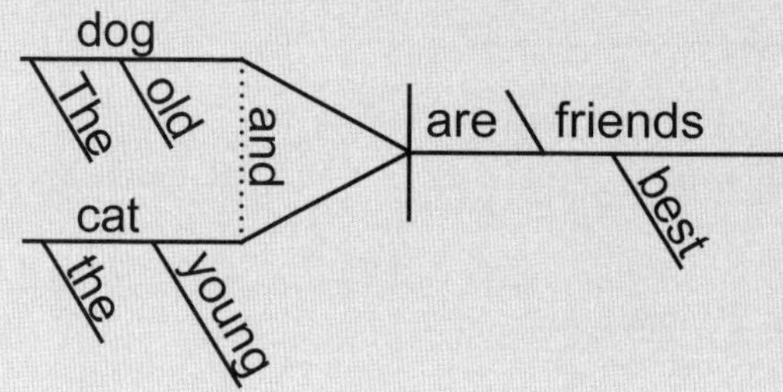

4. Diagram each sentence.

   a. Hector and Paola went sledding yesterday.

   b. My mom and I rode our bikes.

   c. Striped kittens and spotted puppies are my favorites!

   d. Dirty dishes and crusty pots filled the sink.

Lesson 10: Compound Predicates

Compound predicates (two or more verbs) are diagrammed in order, one above the other, with the *coordinating conjunction* joining them together.

The children **danced** *and* **sang**.

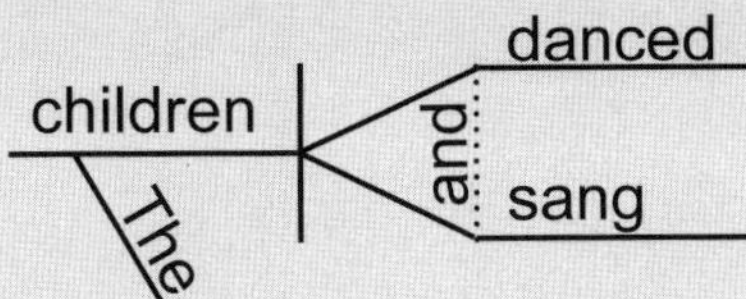

Any adverb modifying a verb is diagrammed below the verb it is modifying.

Sally **spoke** softly and **smiled** sweetly.

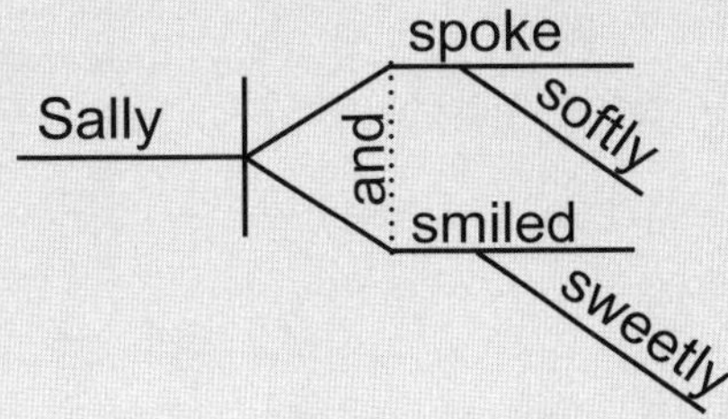

1. Each sentence diagram below has an error. Diagram each sentence correctly.

   a. The squirrels frolicked and played.

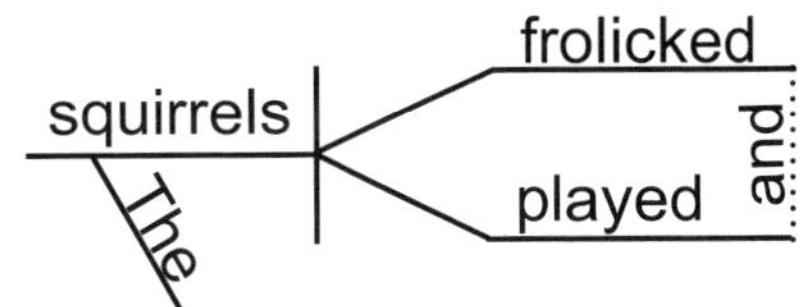

   b. My parakeets chirp and chatter.

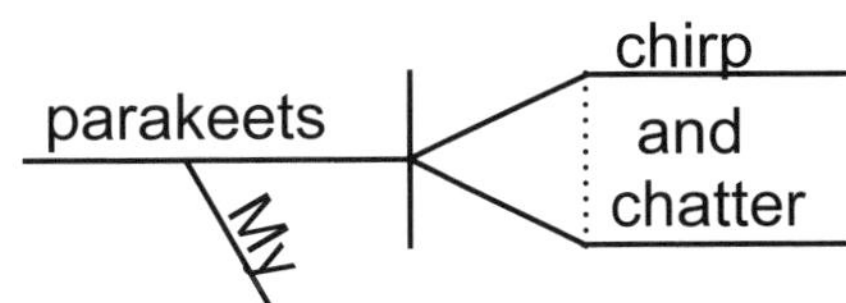

2. Fill in the diagram for each sentence.

a. The hungry baby screamed and cried.

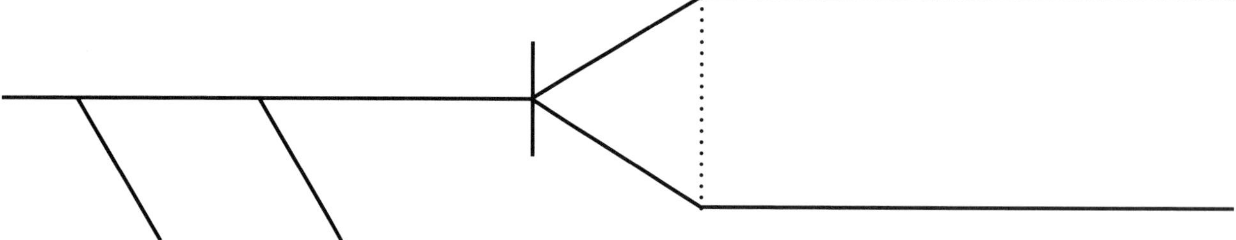

b. Mrs. Valencia prints neatly and draws carefully.

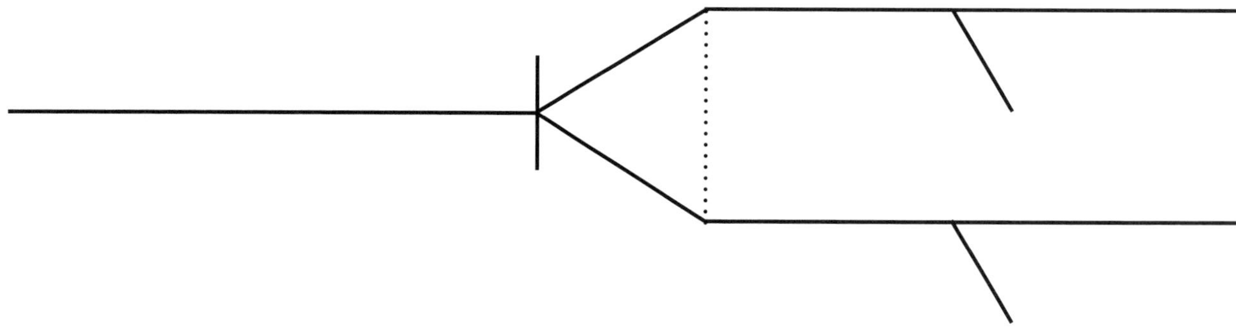

c. The monkeys at the zoo swing lazily but screech nervously.

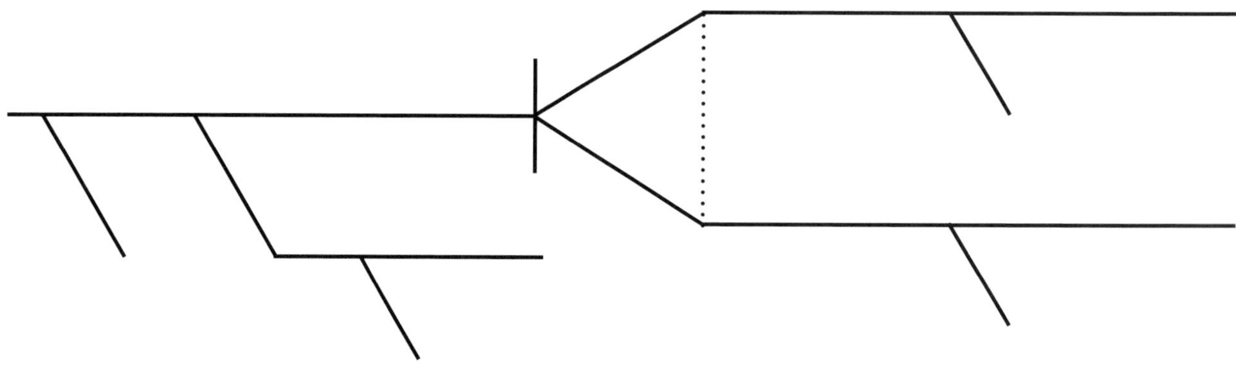

When **compound predicates** each have their own direct objects, diagram each object with its predicate.

Emmie **likes** ballet but **dislikes** jazz.

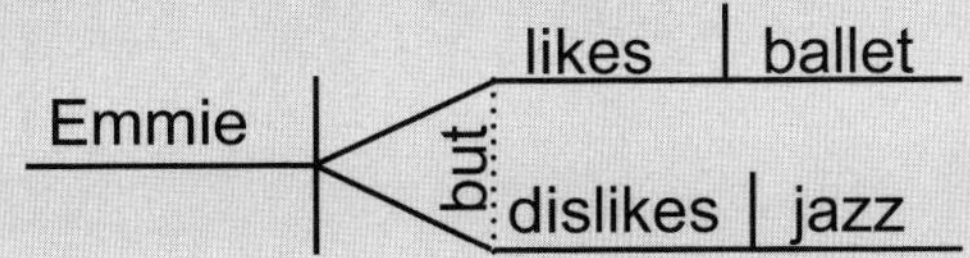

3. Write a sentence to match each diagram. Then complete the diagram.

a. ....

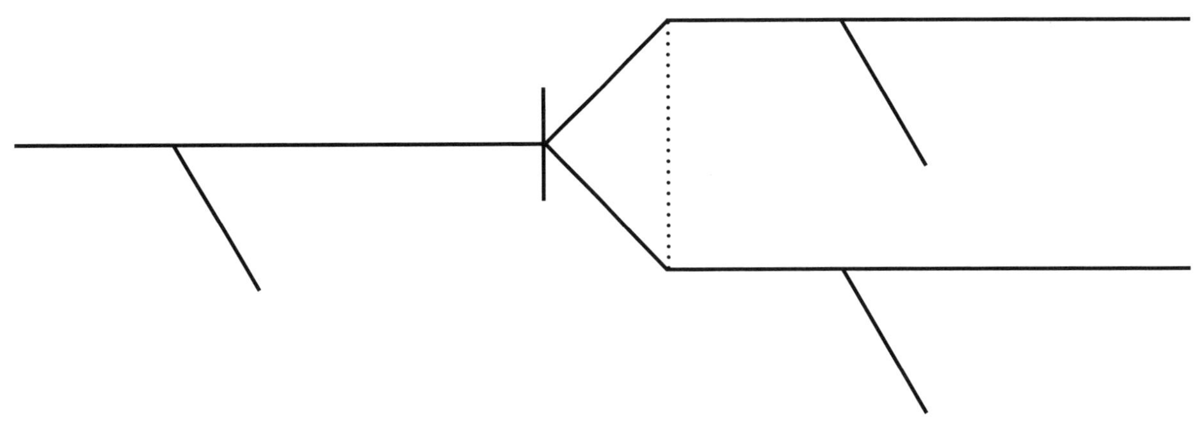

b. ....

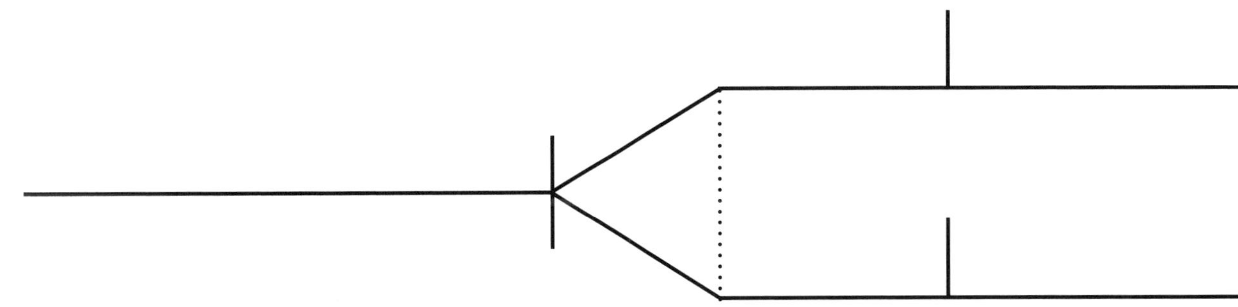

Any **adverb** modifying both *verbs* is diagrammed under the main line before the verbs split.

She *sang* and *danced* **enthusiastically**.

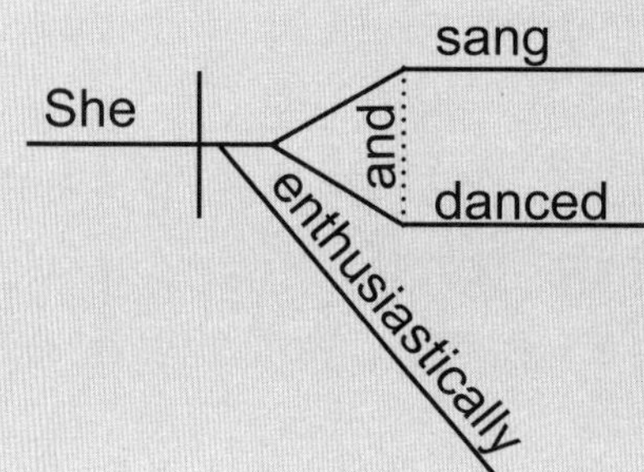

4. Diagram each sentence.

   a. My dog barks and growls.

   b. Some birds fly gracefully but walk clumsily.

   c. Sloths lazily swing and play.

   d. Hippopotami chew slowly but can run fast!

Lesson 11: Compound Direct Objects

A **compound direct object** has more than one direct object for the verb. They are diagrammed on a split line after the verb, with the *coordinating conjunction* joining them together.

I will have **spaghetti** *or* **tortellini**.

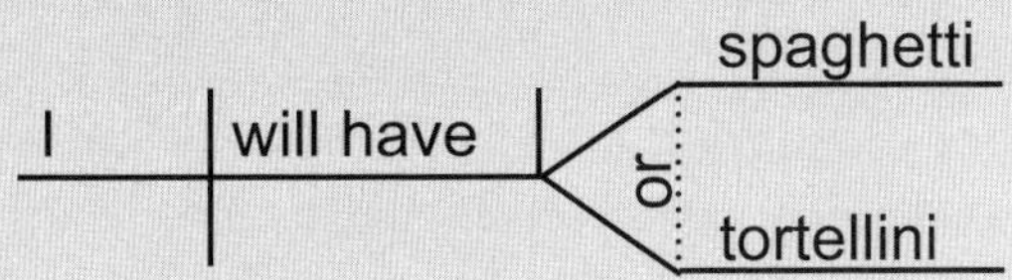

1. Each sentence diagram below has errors. Diagram each sentence correctly.

a. Dad bought lollipops and licorice.

bought lollipops
Dad
and licorice

b. Kyle learned archery and swordplay.

archery
Kyle
learned
and
swordplay

c. Car mechanics use wrenches and screwdrivers.

wrenches
mechanics
use
Car
and
screwdrivers

<u>Adjectives</u> modifying the **direct objects** are diagrammed below the line.

She wore a <u>pretty</u> **skirt** *but* an <u>ugly</u> **blouse**.

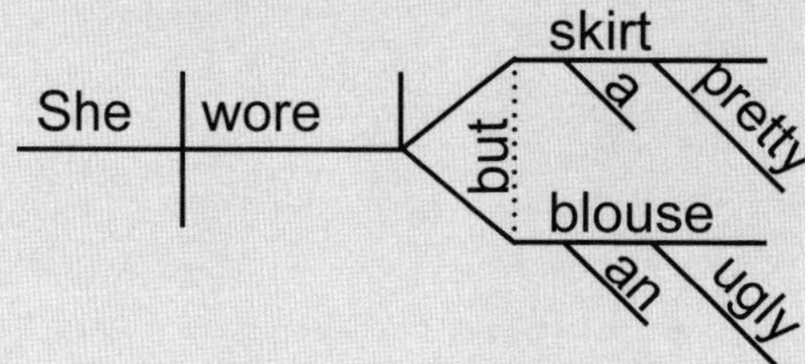

2. Fill in the diagram for each sentence.

a. She cleaned the kitchen and the bathroom.

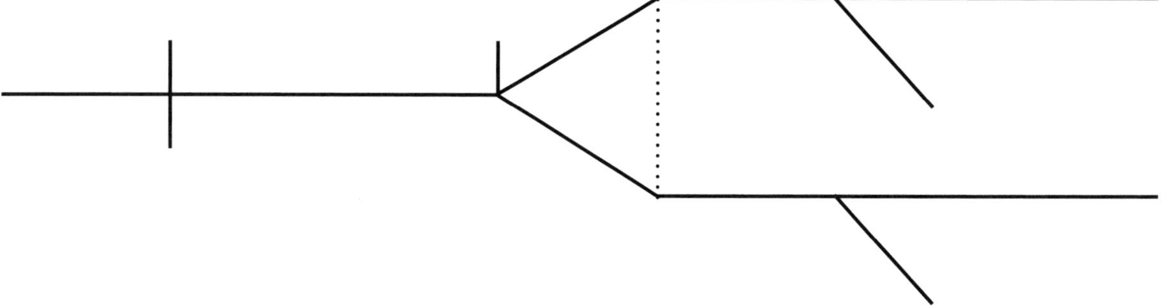

b. They will watch *The Hobbit* or *Star Wars*.

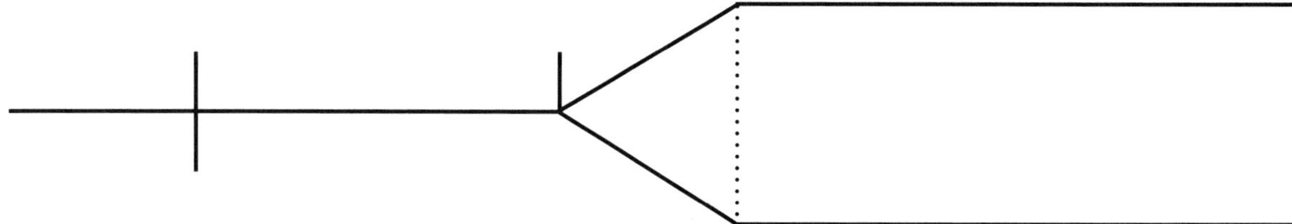

c. She would like sweet tea or iced lemonade.

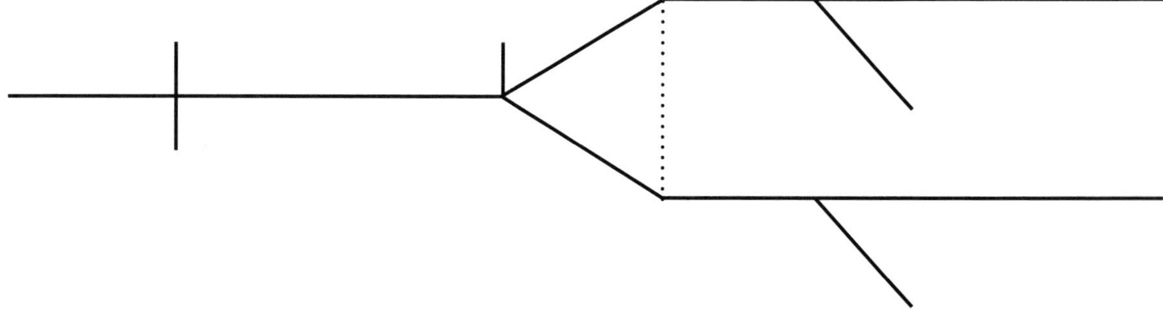

3. Write a sentence to match each diagram, then complete the diagram.

a. ....

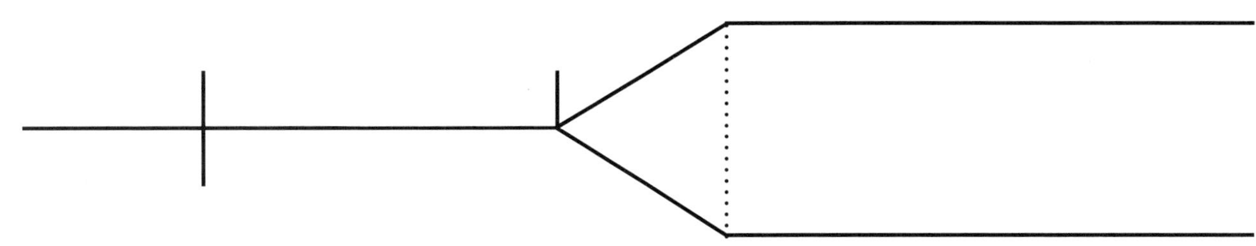

b. ....

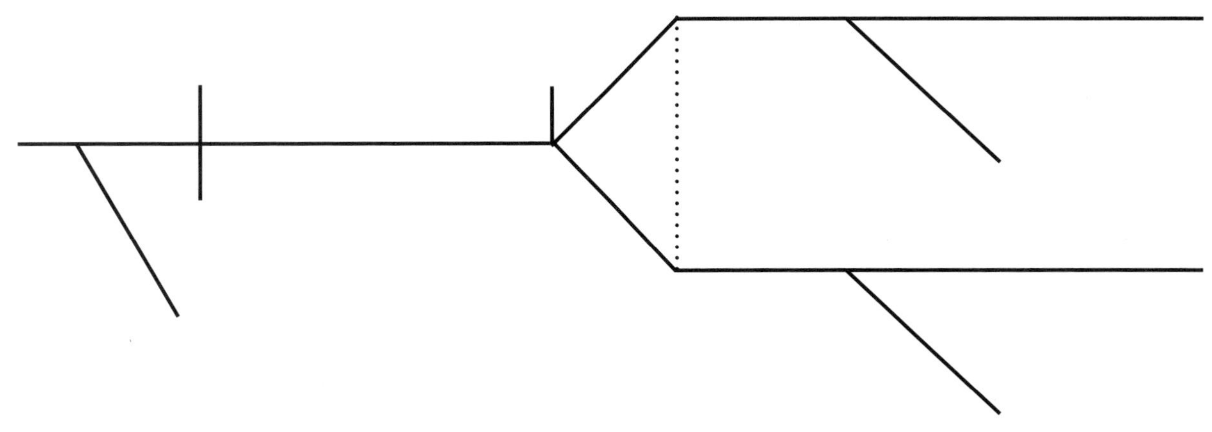

c. ....

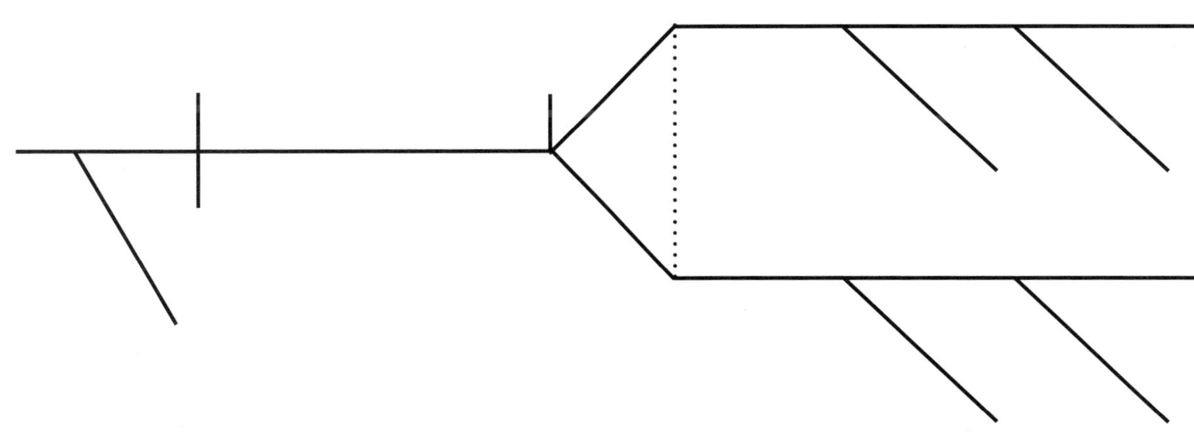

Sometimes one <u>adjective</u> can modify both **direct objects**. It is diagrammed below the main line just before the direct objects.

Elise washed the <u>dirty</u> **pots** *and* **pans**.

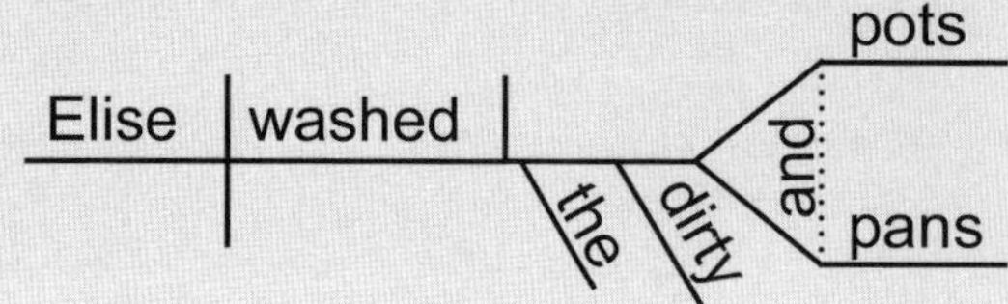

4. Diagram each sentence.

   a. Jaedon wore socks and shoes.

   b. Grace fed the dogs and the rabbits.

   c. Tyler juggled new rings and pins.

   d. Miss Mary planted beautiful red roses and yellow lilies.

Lesson 12: Compound Predicate Adjectives and Nouns

When two or more adjectives or nouns that modify the subject come after a *linking verb* (is, am, are, was, were), they are **compound predicate adjectives** or **compound predicate nouns**. They are diagrammed after the verb, separated by a slanted line.

The puppies *are* **playful** and **energetic**!

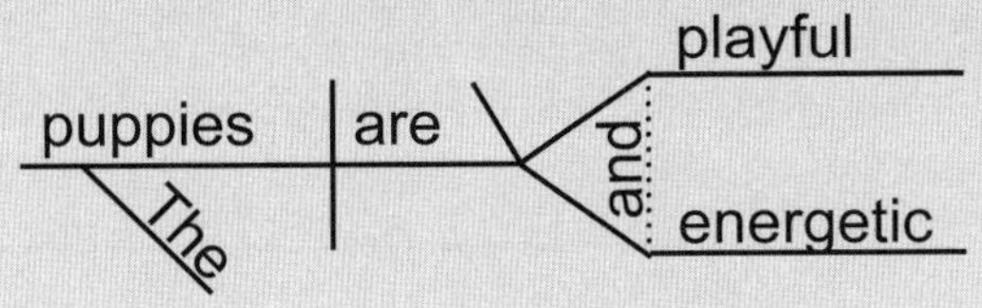

Mrs. Gonzales *is* my **teacher** and our **friend**.

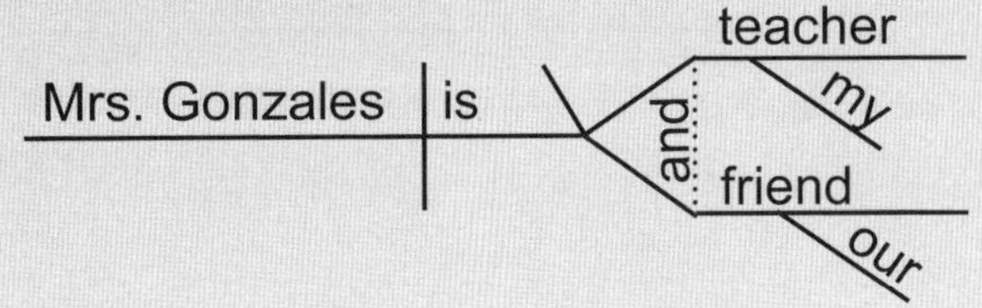

1. Each sentence diagram below has errors. Diagram each sentence correctly.

   a. Her flowers are beautiful and fragrant.

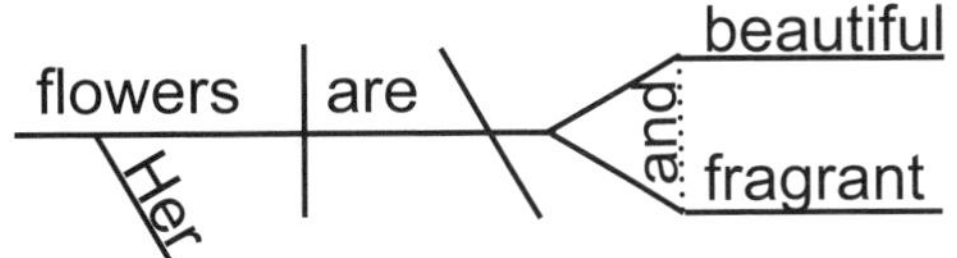

   b. Bugs Bunny is smart but silly.

Bugs Bunny is
smart
but
silly

2. Fill in the diagram for each sentence.

a. Charlie was scared and nervous.

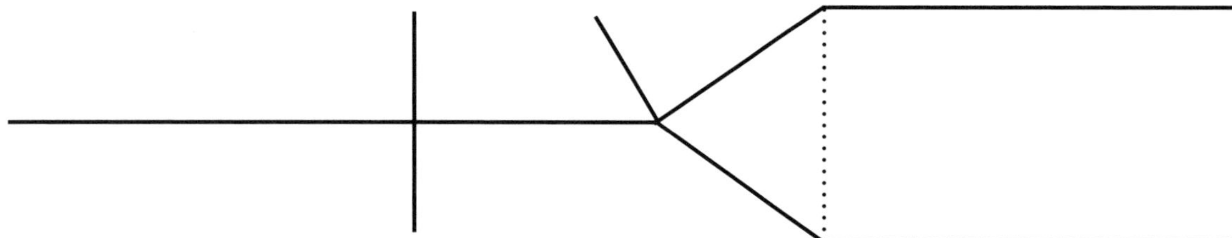

b. He is an actor and a musician.

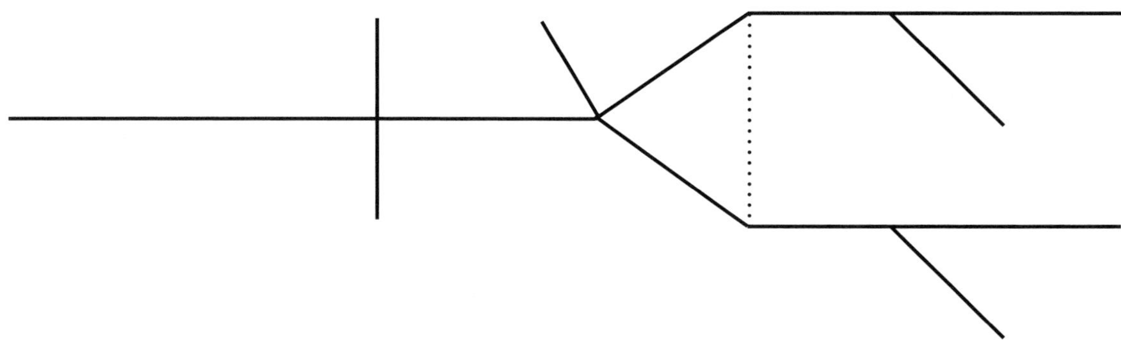

c. Mr. Simms is a history teacher and a soccer coach.

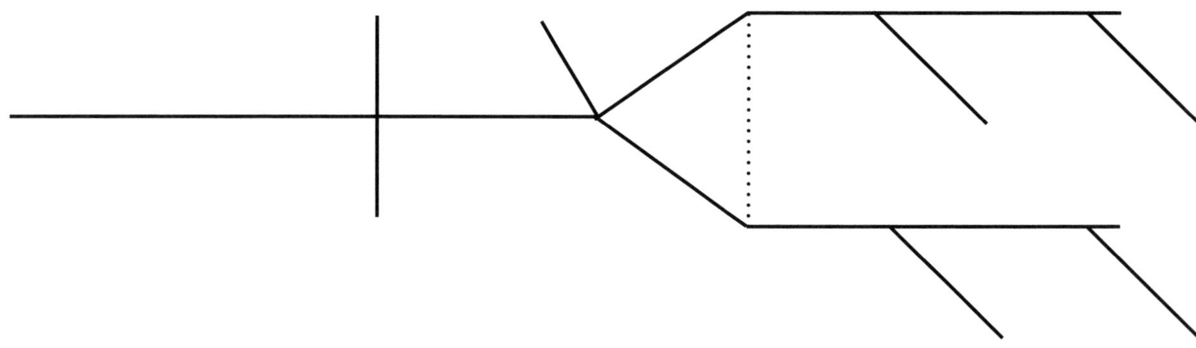

Sometimes an **adjective** can modify (describe) both predicate nouns. It is diagrammed below the main line just before the predicate nouns.

They are **funny** entertainers and musicians.

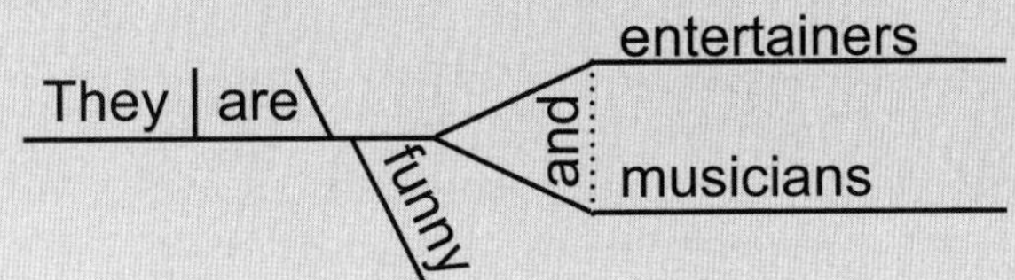

3. Write a sentence to match each diagram. Then complete the diagram.

a. ....

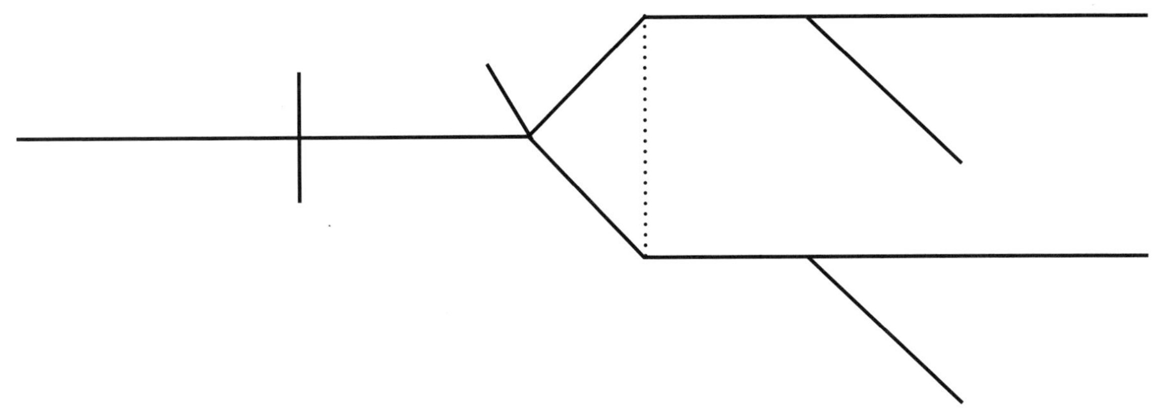

b. ....

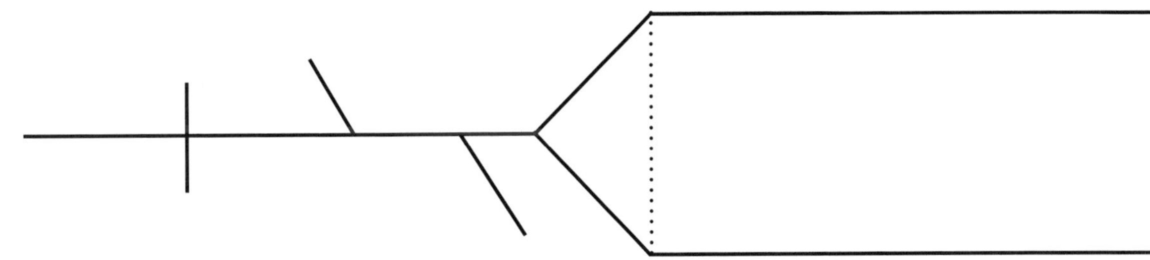

Three or more items separated by commas are diagrammed in order, one above the other, with the *coordinating conjunction* joining them together.

Ashley, Amanda, *and* Adriana are triplets.

Ashley
Amanda
and
Adriana
are
triplets

They own horses, cats, *and* dogs.

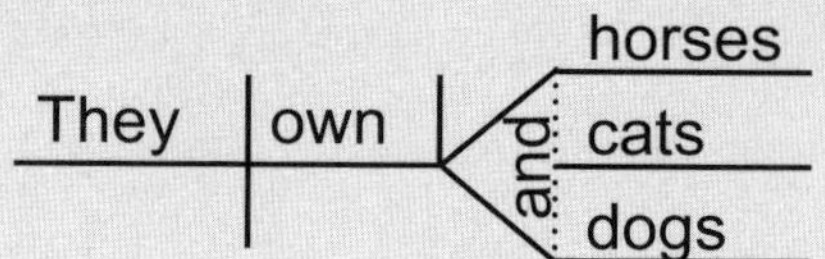

4. Diagram each sentence.

   a. Ryan is tall, thin, and handsome.

   b. Parents, teachers, and students enjoyed the performances.

   c. Joey, Jimmy, and Alexandria walked the dog.

   d. Emily is a dancer, a singer, and an actress.

Review

Diagram each of these sentences.

1. President Washington died.

2. Benjamin Franklin discovered electricity.

3. Johanna Spyri wrote *Heidi*.

4. Abraham Lincoln wore a top hat.

5. The brave and strong soldier saved us.

6. The baby kangaroo joyfully bounced.

7. The young nanny spoke gently but firmly.

8. Percy Jackson is a demi-god.

9. My cousin is she.

10. Tom Sawyer was mischievous!

11. Mom's cell phone is broken.

12. The purple shovels in the sandbox are new.

13. Carlena bought the flowered shirt on the hanger.

14. Ann Marie hung her coat in the closet.

15. They will sing with the choir before the concert.

16. Collin and Julia are siblings.

17. My old dog and your new puppy like the same treats.

18. The old car engine spurts and splutters.

19. The band played well and sang beautifully.

20. Goats eat grass and shoelaces.

21. He sold the old skis and boots.

22. Willy Wonka made delicious chocolates and tasty gumballs.

23. Amy is patient and kind.

24. Meg, Jo, Beth, and Amy are Little Women.

25. The friendly waitress quickly delivered delicious chips, salsa, and guacomole.

Answers

Lesson 1 (pp. 1-4)

1 a. 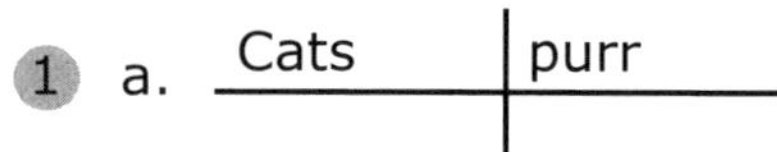
Cats | purr

b. Chickens | cluck

c. Artists | draw

2 a. Flowers | grow

b. Emily | should read

c. She | sneezed

d. They | had eaten

3 Sentences will vary. Examples:

a. Cows moo. Cows | moo

b. I cried. I | cried

c. Michael can swim. Michael | can swim

d. Fireworks exploded! Fireworks | exploded

4 a. Mimi | bakes

b. He | has spoken

c. Mr. Cavanaugh | tripped

d. Grandma Polly | will visit

Lesson 2 (pp. 5-8)

1 a. Joey | is playing | cards

b. We | baked | cupcakes

c. Uncle Mike | has eaten | squid

2 a. Bees | make | honey

b. Uncle Fred | builds | cars

c. Mrs. McDonald | teaches | preschool

d. Principal Suarez | wears | suits

3 Sentences will vary. Examples:

a. Elephants eat peanuts.

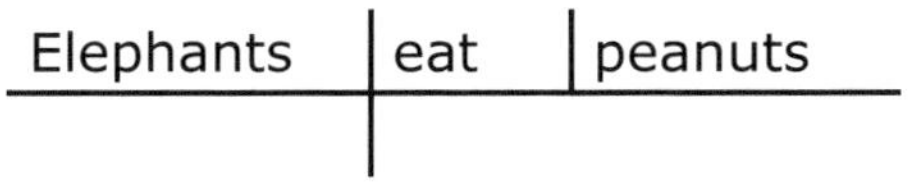

Elephants	eat	peanuts

b. Superman hates kryptonite.

Superman	hates	kryptonite

c. Ms. Louise makes sushi.

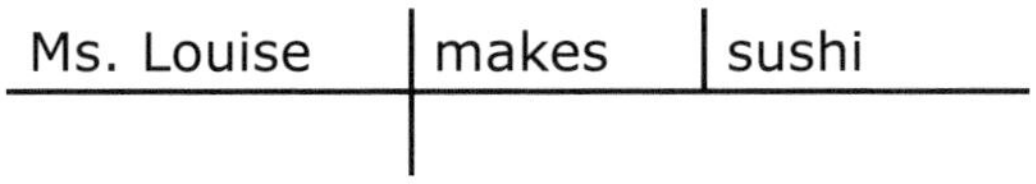

Ms. Louise	makes	sushi

d. We played soccer.

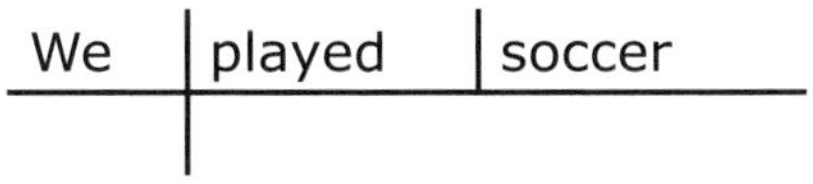

We	played	soccer

4 a.

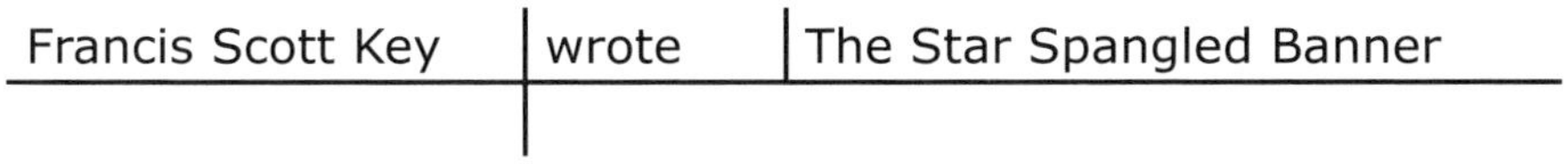

Francis Scott Key	wrote	The Star Spangled Banner

b.

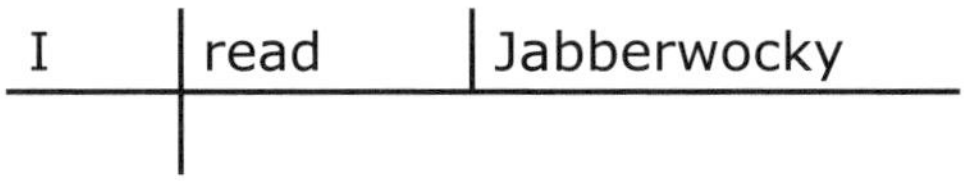

I	read	Jabberwocky

c.

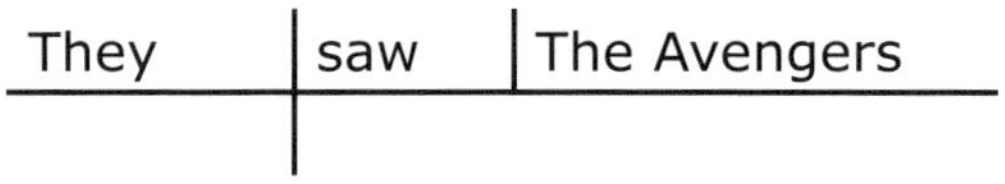

They	saw	The Avengers

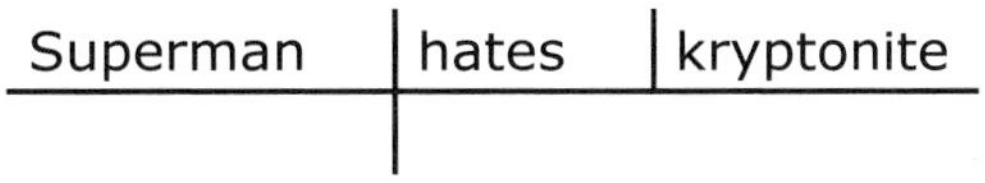

d.

Aunt Cindy	will watch	Cinderella

Lesson 3 (pp. 9-12)

1 a.

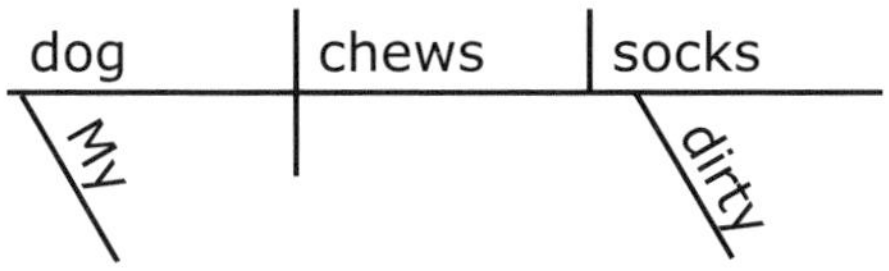

dog	chews	socks
My		dirty

b.

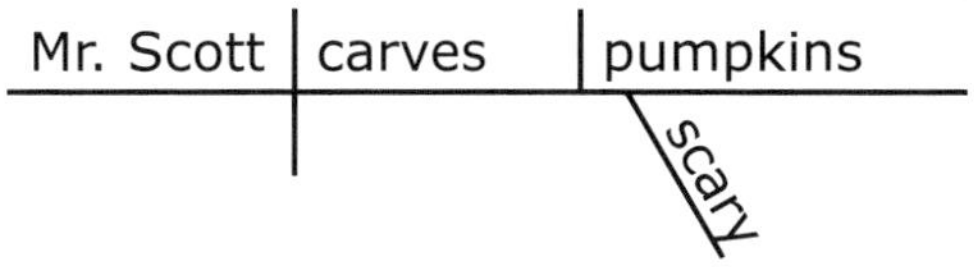

Mr. Scott	carves	pumpkins
		scary

c.

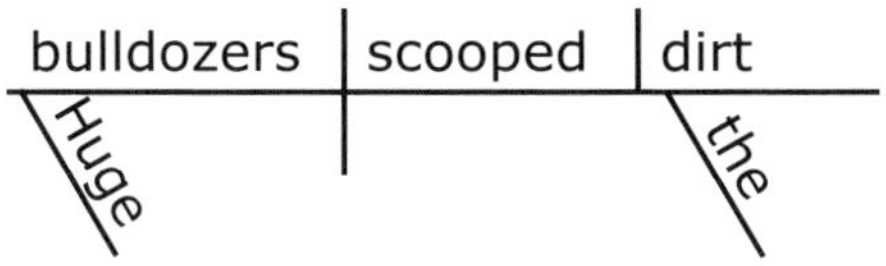

bulldozers	scooped	dirt
Huge		the

2 a.

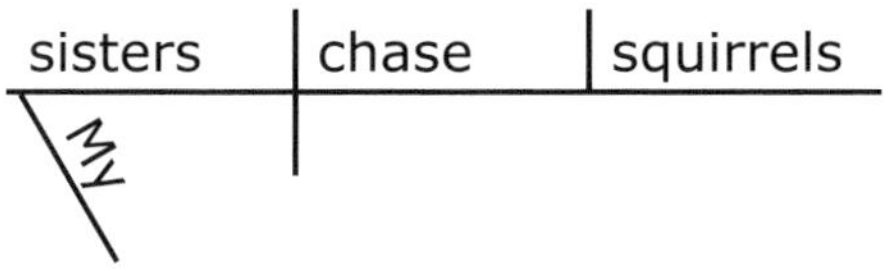

sisters	chase	squirrels
My		

b.

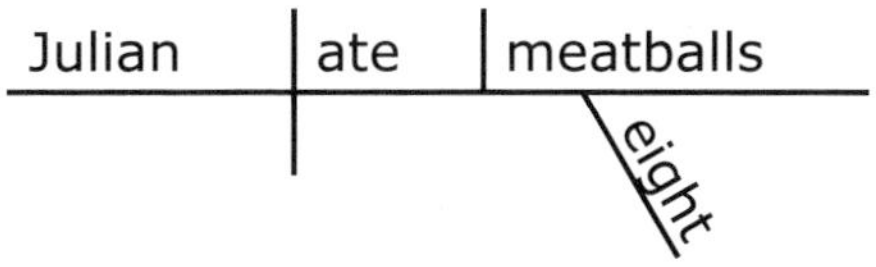

Julian	ate	meatballs
		eight

c.

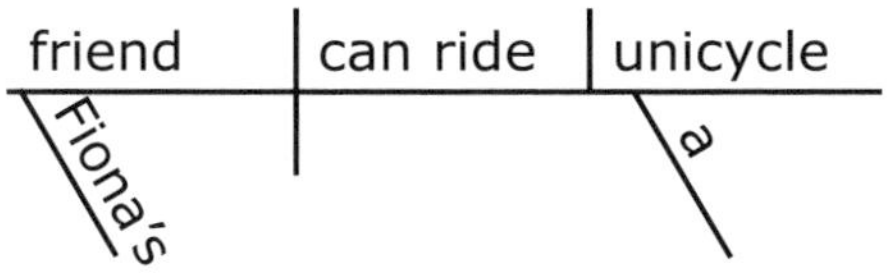

friend	can ride	unicycle
Fiona's		a

3 Sentences will vary. Examples:

a. Many vikings carry a shield.

vikings | carry | shield
Many
a

b. The brown and white hamster eats colored paper.

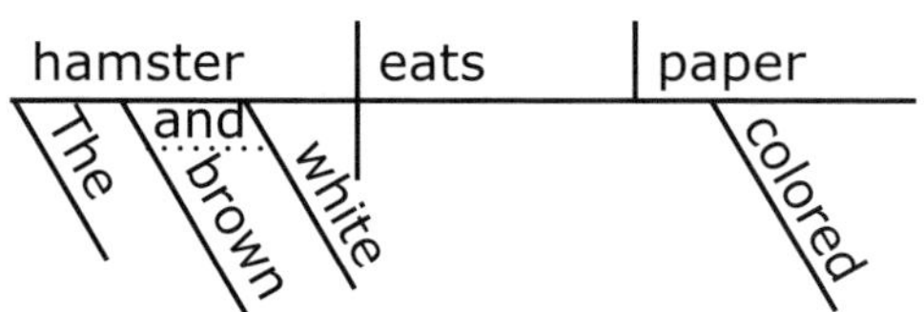

4 a.

swans | are swimming
Seven

b.

goat | ate | shoes
Your
and
hungry
smelly
my
new

c.

I | bought | flag
a
but
used
clean
American

d.

carrier | delivered | cards
The
mail
five
birthday

Lesson 4 (pp. 13-16)

1 a.

Mr. Sanchez | sneezes
often

b.

granny | sews
My
well

c.

kittens | mewed
The
tiny
softly

2 a.

Dad | slurps | soup
loudly

b.

birds | flew
Three
gracefully

3 Sentences will vary. Examples:

a. Most teachers print neatly.

teachers | print
Most
neatly

b. My mom quickly washes dishes daily.

mom | washes | dishes
My
quickly
daily

c. Eagles soar grandly and gracefully.

Eagles | soar
and
grandly
gracefully

4 a.

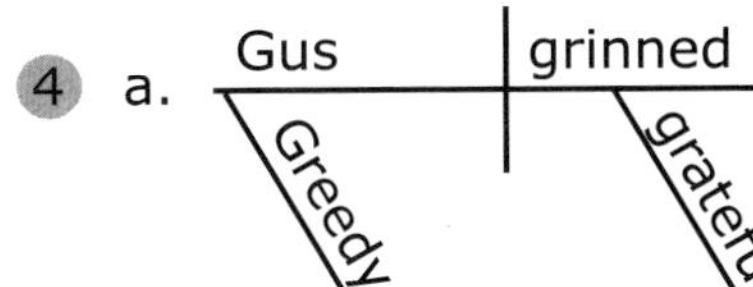

b. Queen Quilla | ate | quince
Quietly
her

c.

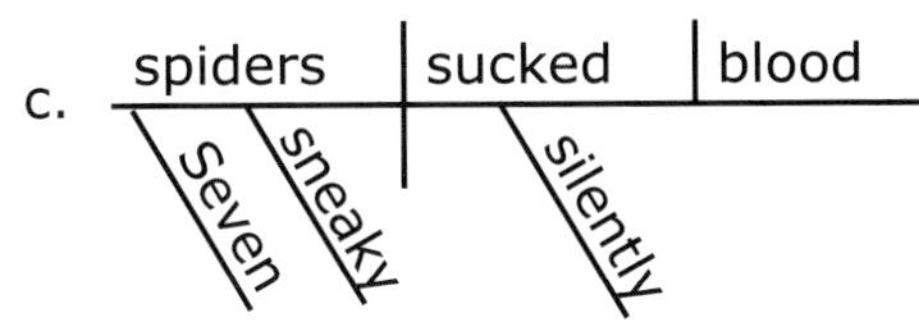

d.

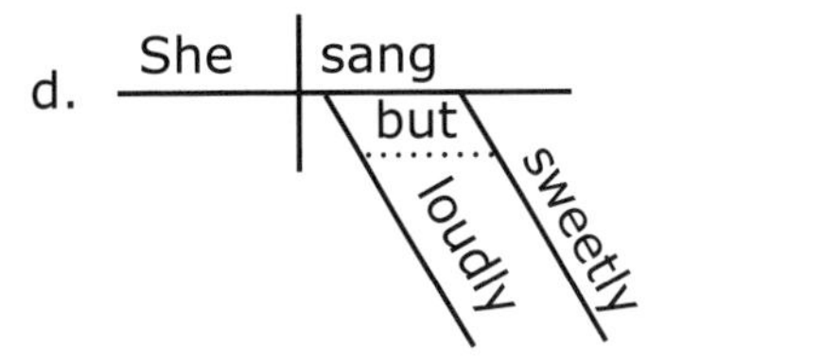

Lesson 5 (pp. 17-20)

1 a.

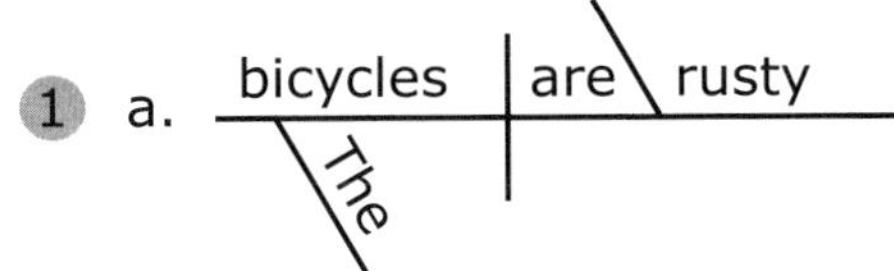

b. Li Wei | is \ Chinese

2 a. c.

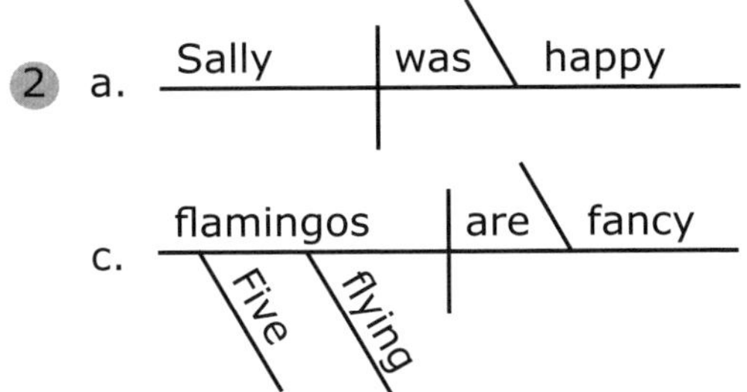

b.

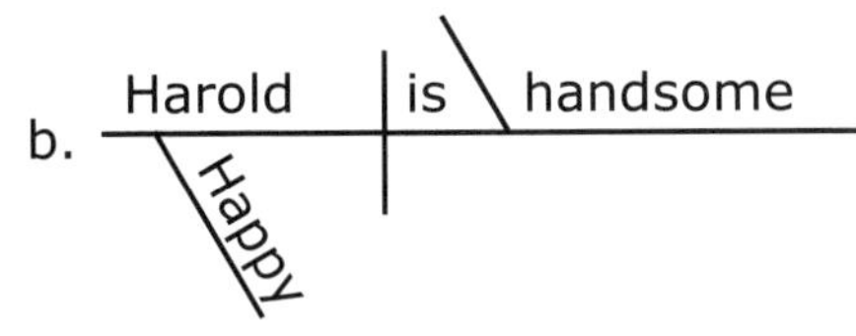

3 Sentences will vary. Examples:

a. Broccoli is yummy. Broccoli | is \ yummy

b. The baby is tired. baby | is \ tired
The

c. Patty's pink petunias are pretty. petunias | are \ pretty
Patty's
pink

4 a. c.

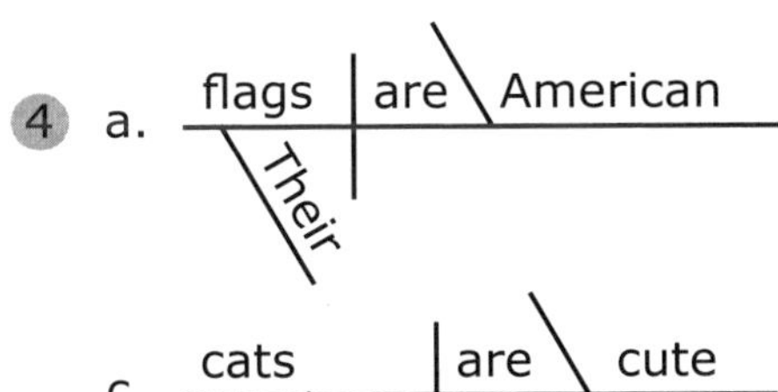

b. d.

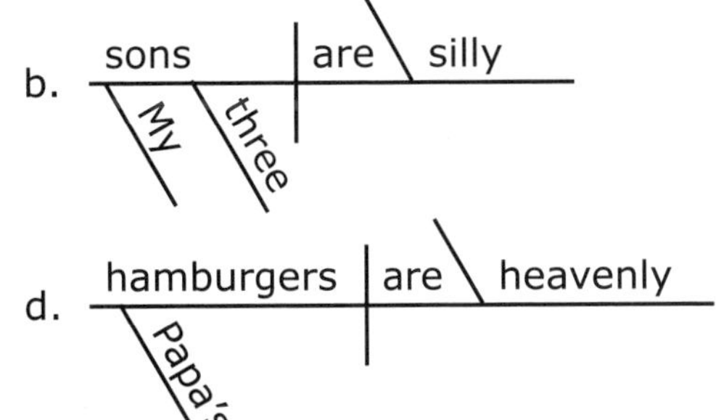

Lesson 6 (pp. 21-24)

1 a.
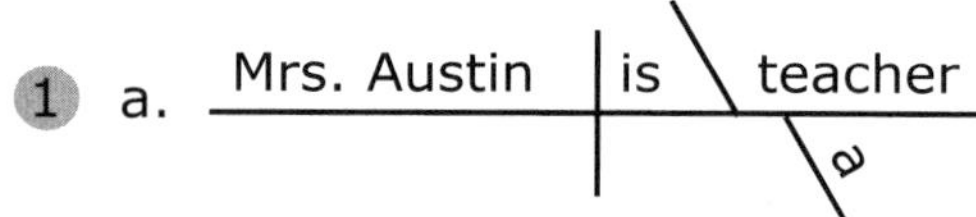

b. I | am \ teenager
a

2 a.
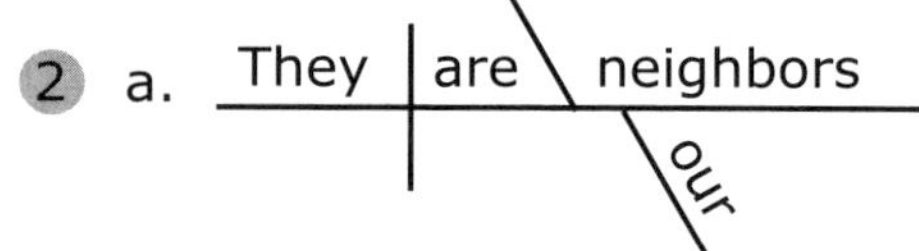

b.
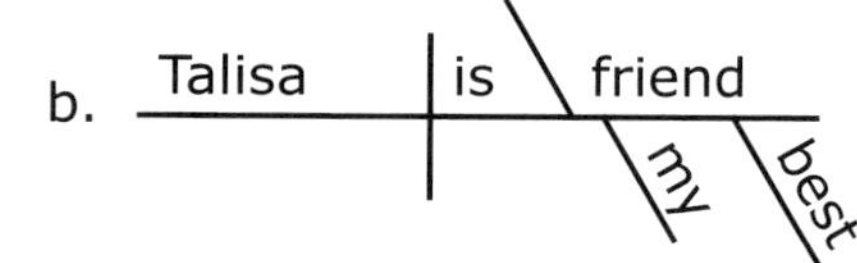

c.
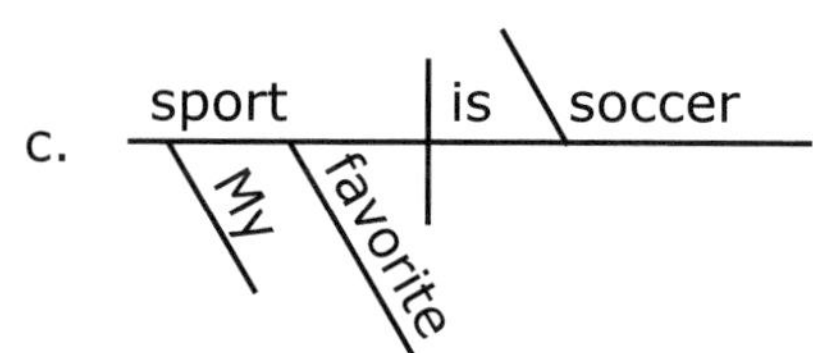

3 Sentences will vary. Examples:

a. My sister is a cheerleader.

sister | is \ cheerleader
My
a

b. Fido is a good dog.

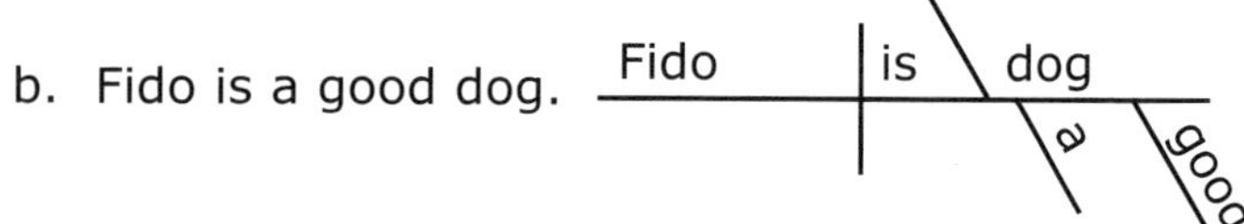

c. Her little brothers were superheroes.

brothers | were \ superheroes
Her
little

4 a.
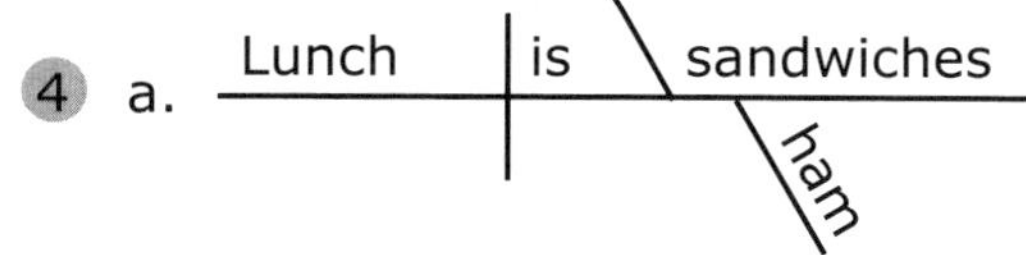

b. cookies | are \ gift
The
sugar
your

c. leader | was \ she
Our
first
scout

d. kittens | were \ friends
The
two
crazy
best

Lesson 7 (pp. 25-28)

1 a.
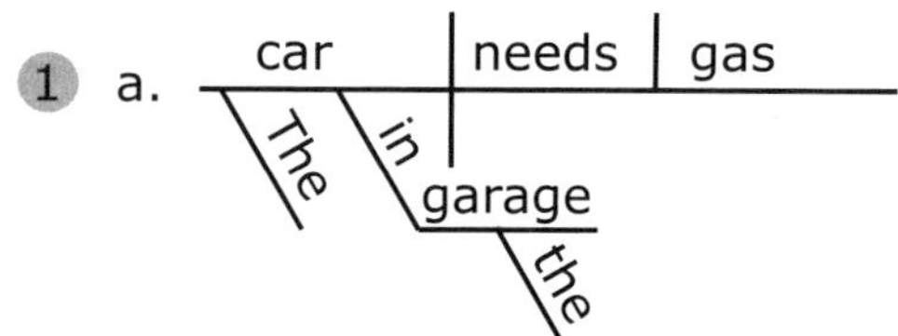

b. piano | is \ old
The
in
corner
the

2 a.

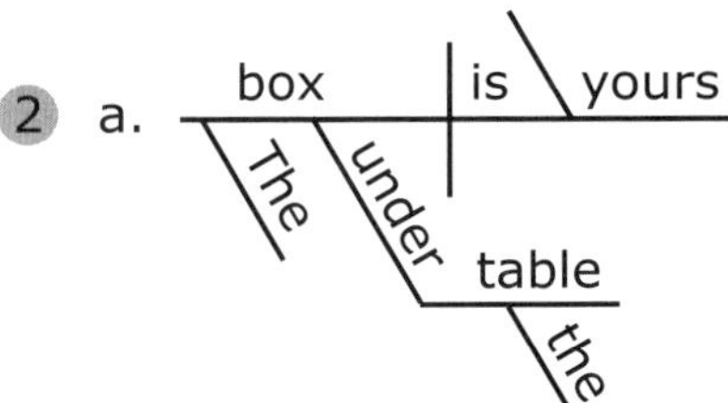

b.

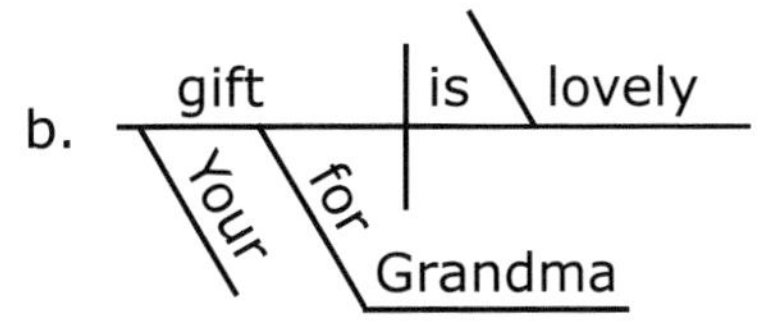

c.

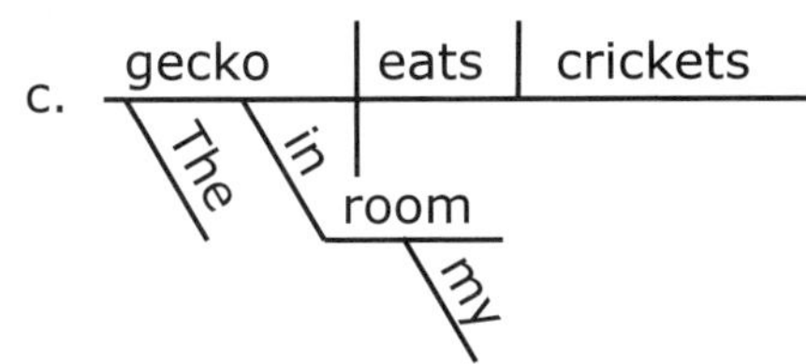

3 Sentences will vary. Examples:

a. The owl in the cage is Harry's.

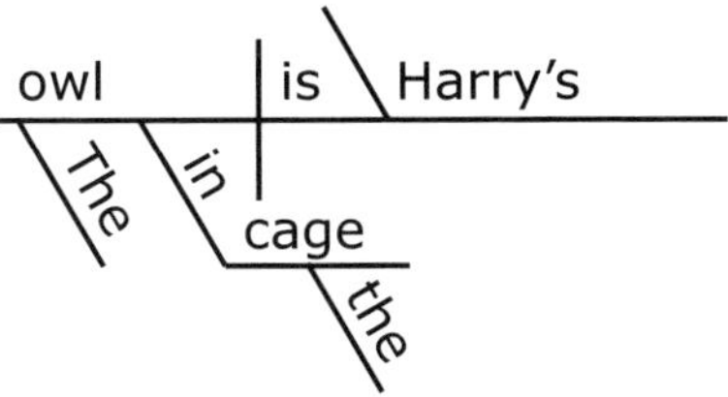

b. The card from Aunt Silvie was inspiring.

card | was \ inspiring
The
from
Aunt Silvie

c. The bee by Tony stung me!

bee | stung | me
The
by
Tony

4 a.

vase | is \ antique
The
on
shelf
the
an

b.

day | was \ fun
Our
at
beach
the

c.

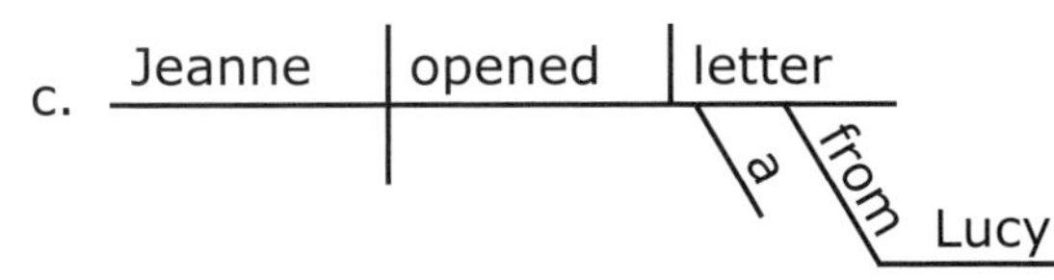

d.

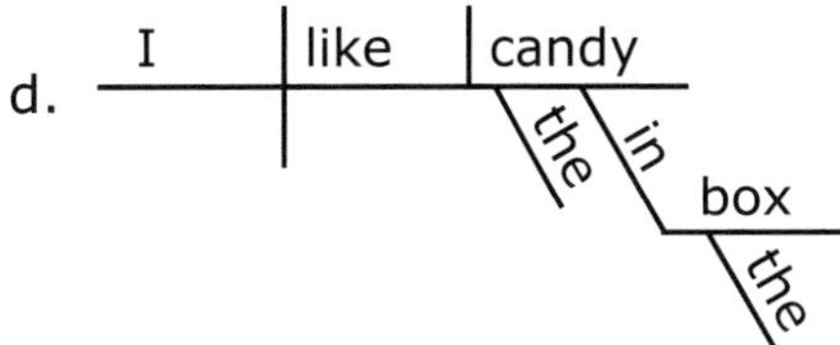

Lesson 8 (pp. 29-32)

1 a.

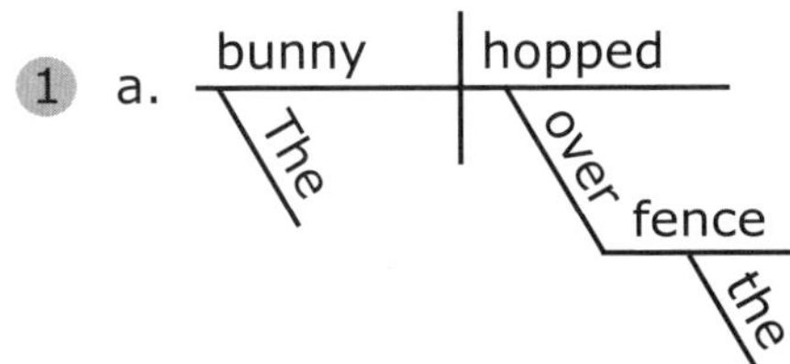

b.

Mom | put | turkey
in
oven
the
the

2 a.

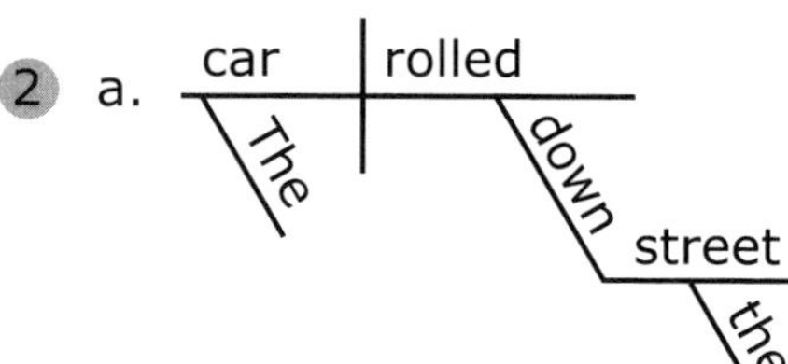

b.

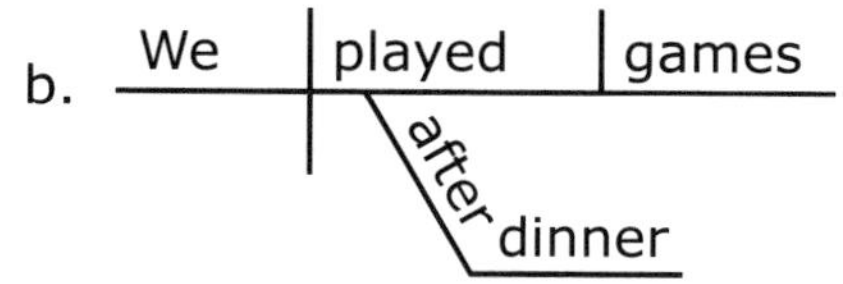

c.

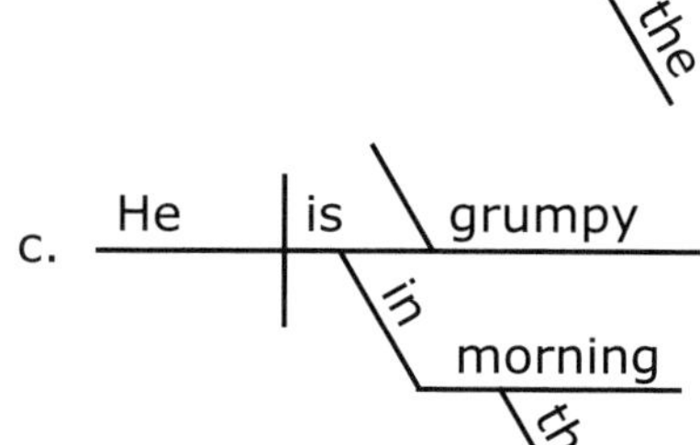

3 Sentences will vary. Examples:

a. Ten peacocks ran around the park.

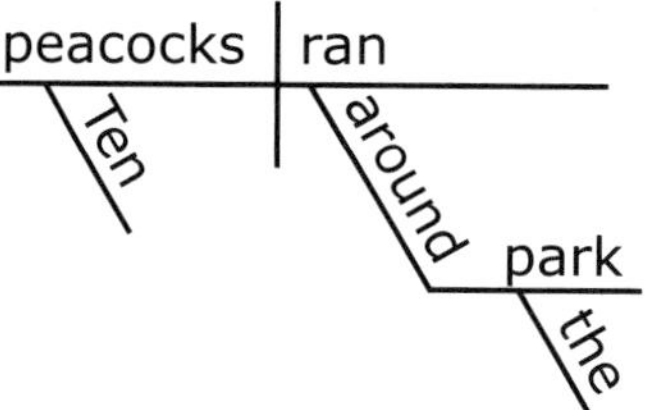

b. We ate popcorn during the movie.

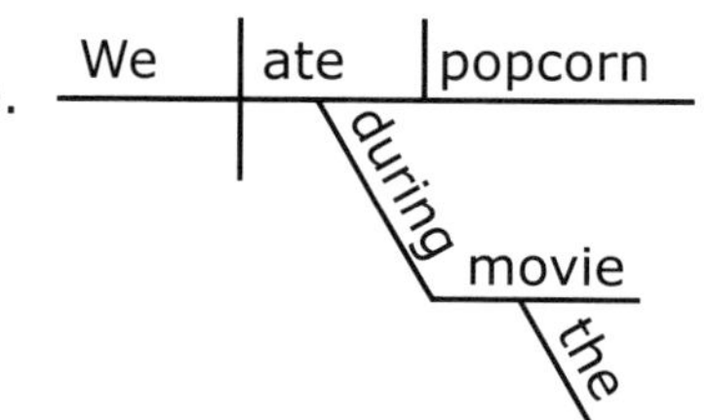

c. We played at the playground before school.

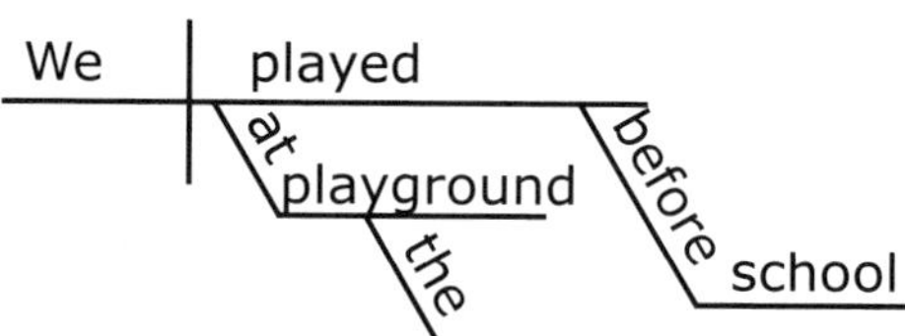

4 a.

flag
fluttered
The
in
breeze
the

b.

They
will sing
Happy Birthday
before
dessert

c.

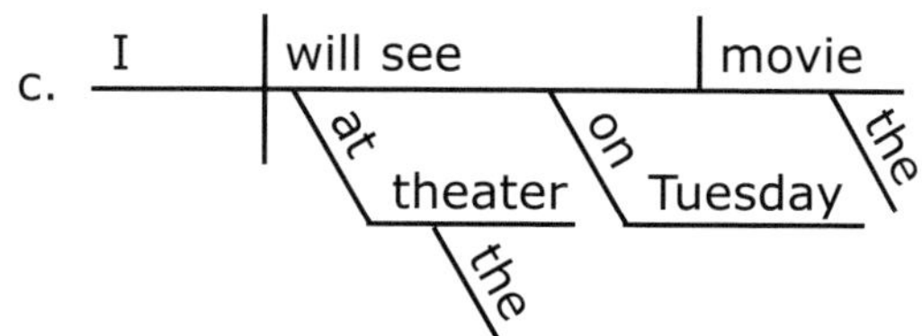

d.

Patrick
reads
books
in
room
his
at
night

Lesson 9 (pp. 33-36)

1 a.

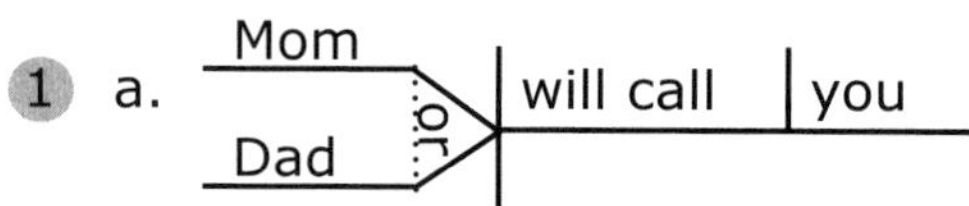

b.

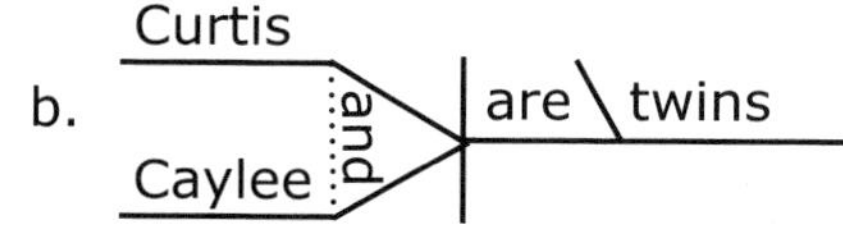

2 a.

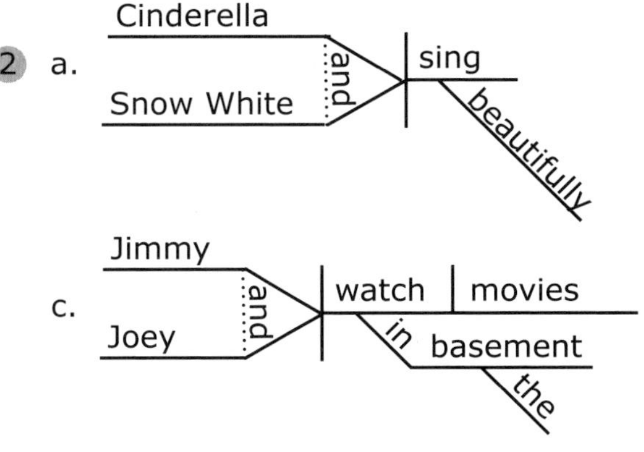

b.

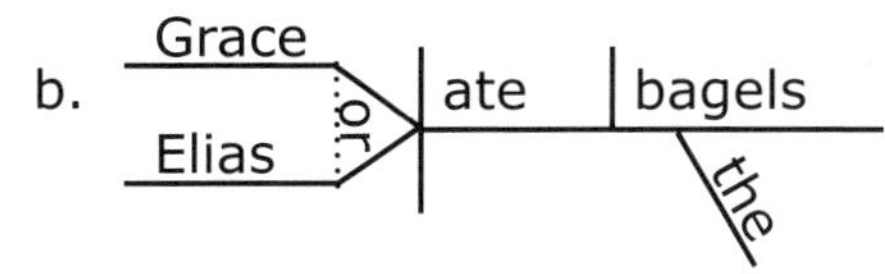

3 Sentences will vary. Examples:

a. Hector and Faolin play soccer.

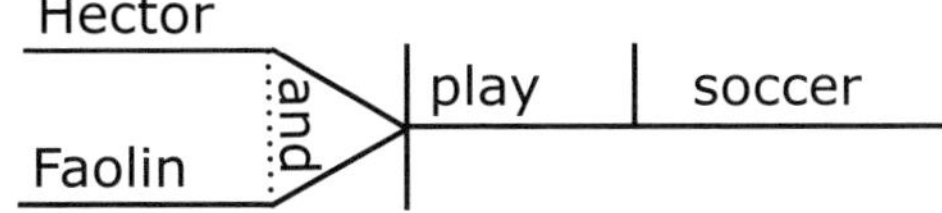

b. Charlie and Teddy are girls.

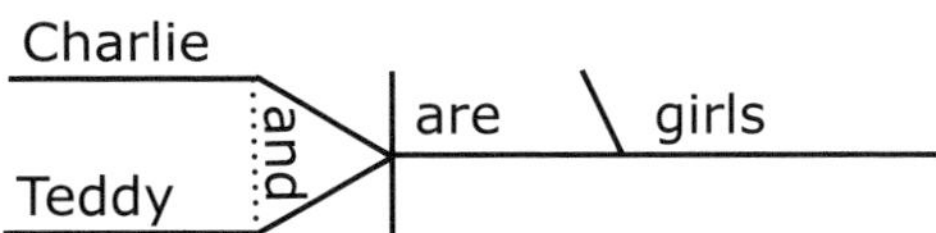

c. Raymond, Andrew, and Josh bought expensive fireworks.

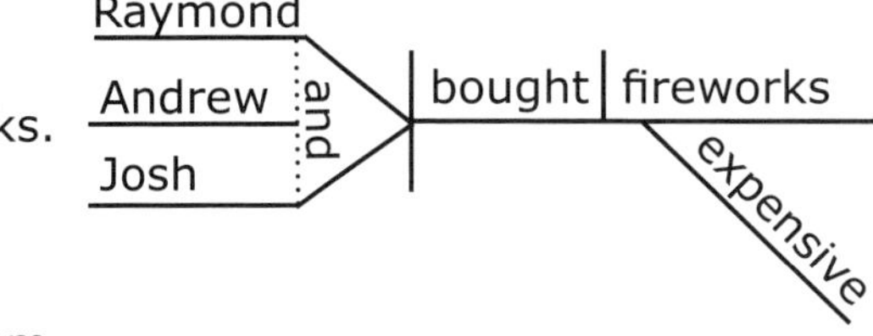

4 a.

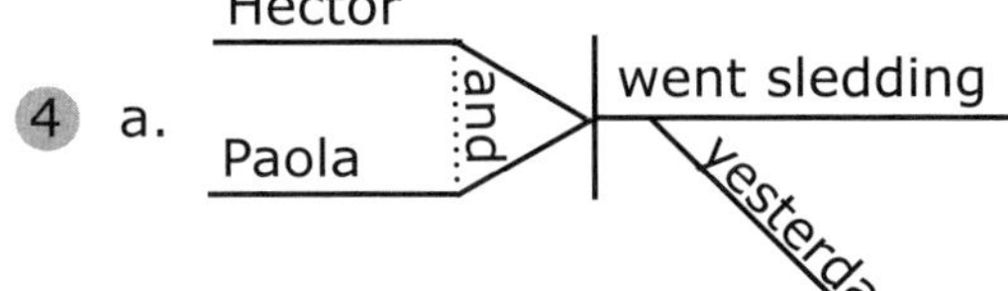

b.

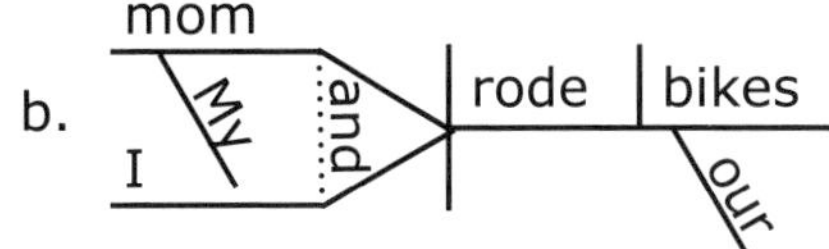

c.

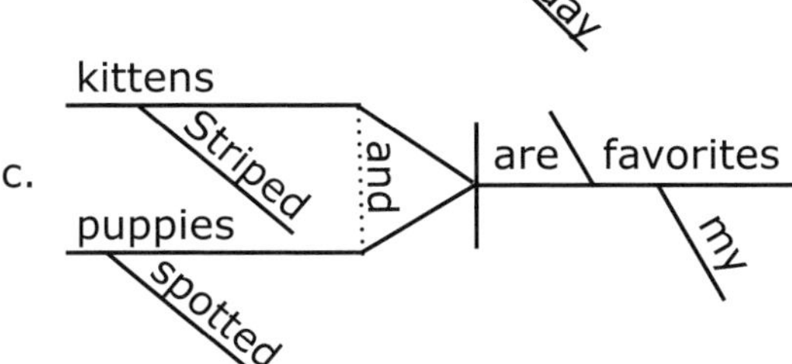

d.

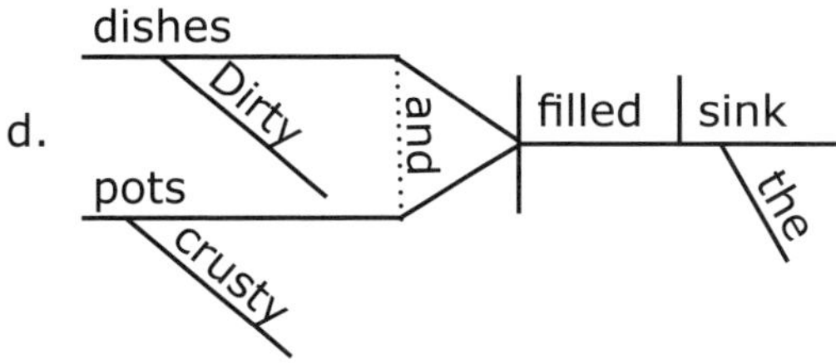

Lesson 10 (pp. 37-40)

1 a.

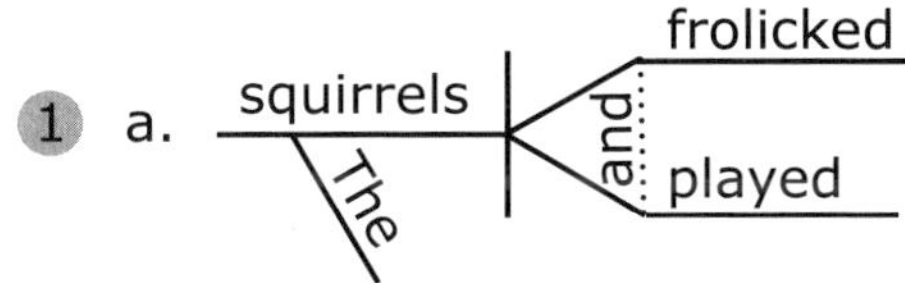

b.

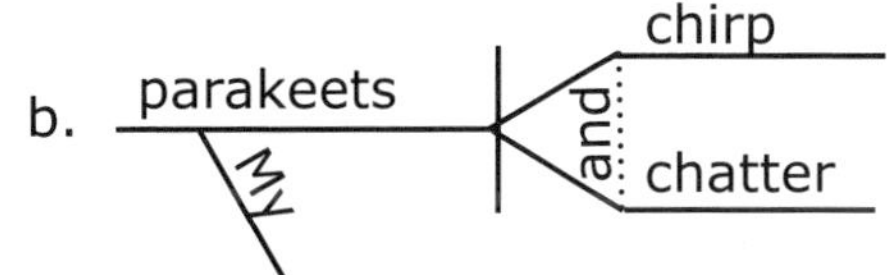

2 a.

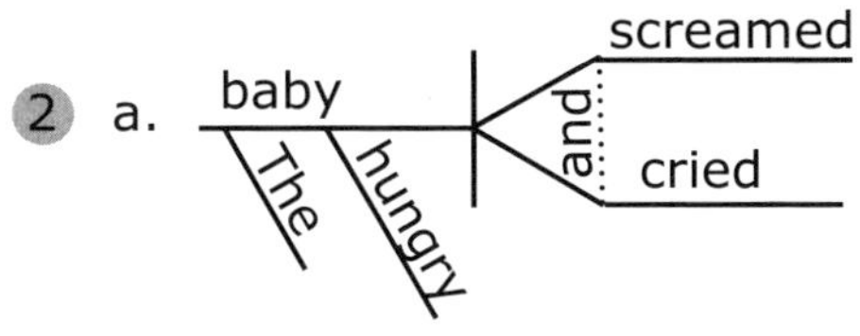

b.

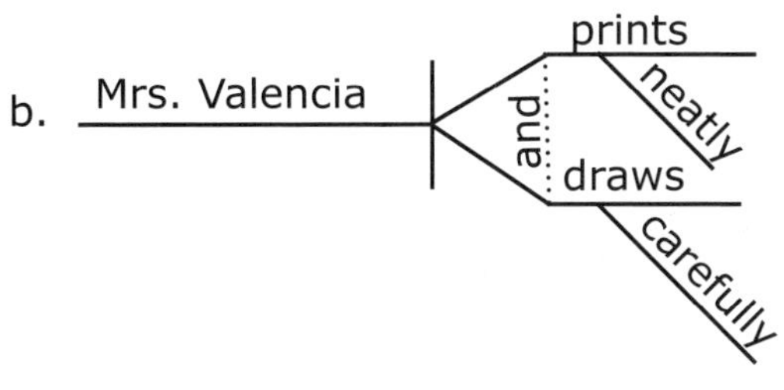

c. 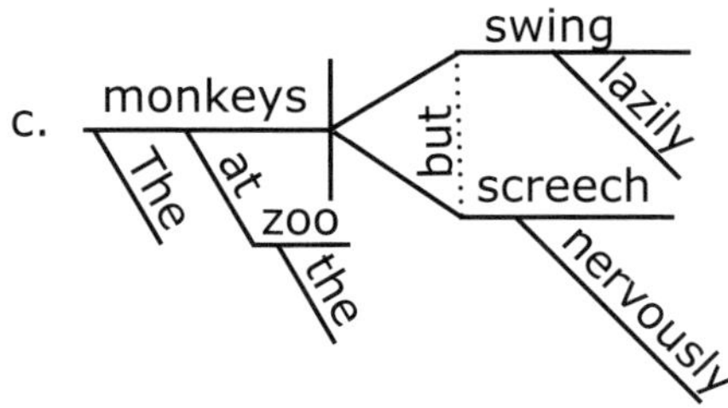

3 Sentences will vary. Examples:

a. The fox leaped gracefully and ran swiftly. 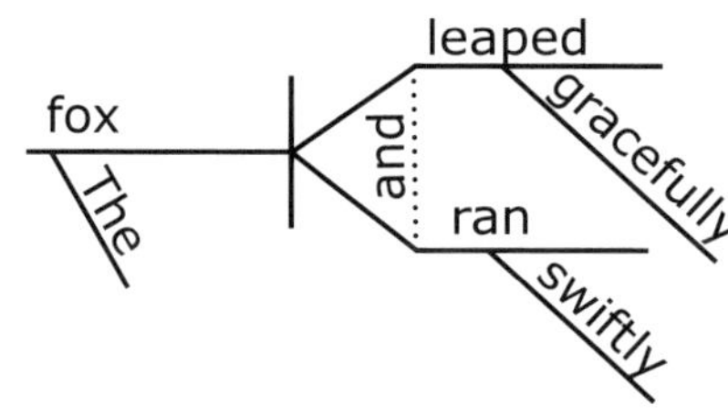

b. Mrs. Baker bakes cookies and sells them. 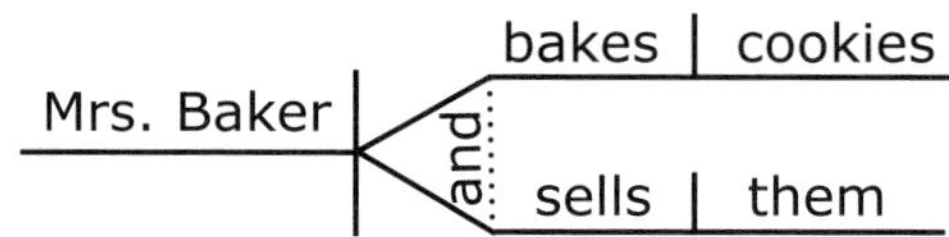

4 a. 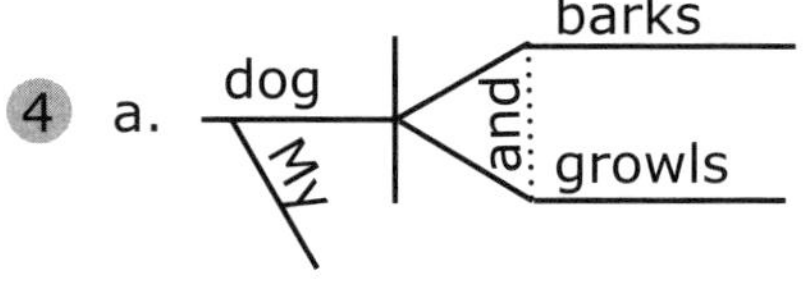

b. 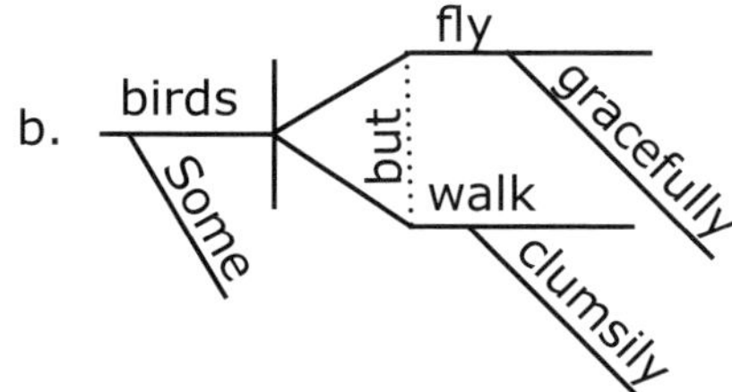

c. 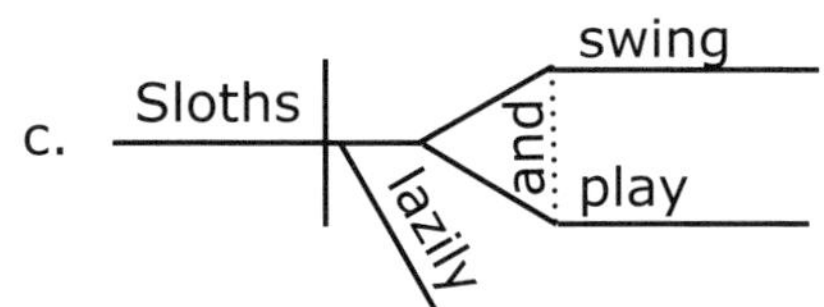

d. 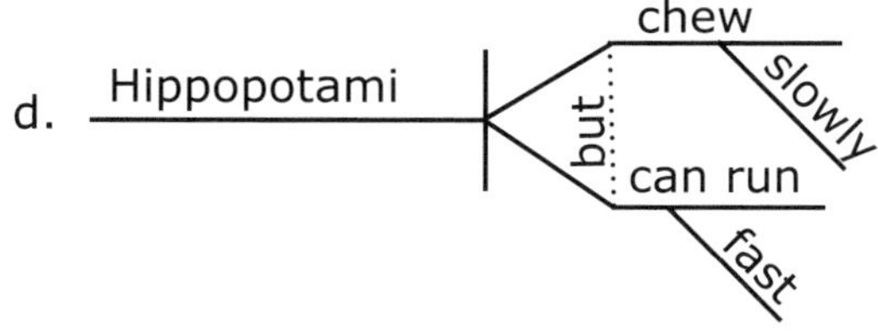

Lesson 11 (pp. 41-44)

1 a. 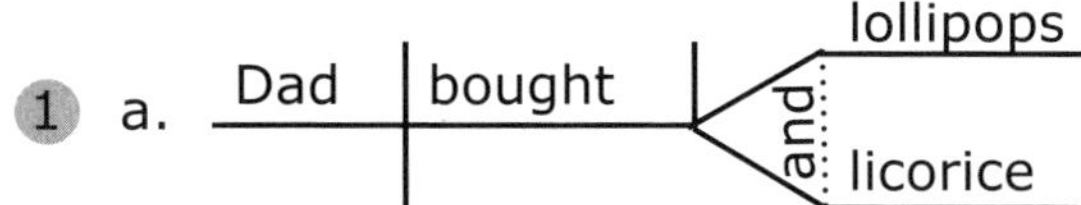

b. 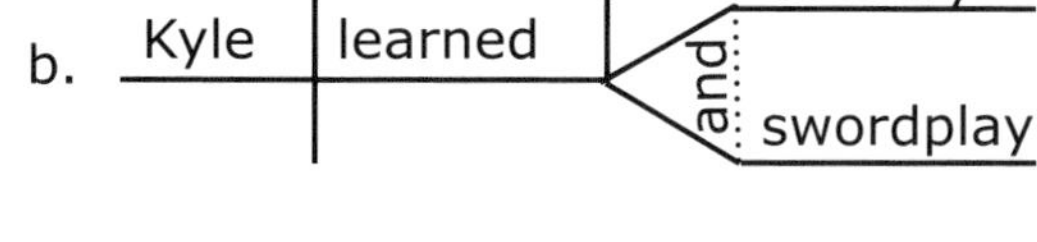

c. 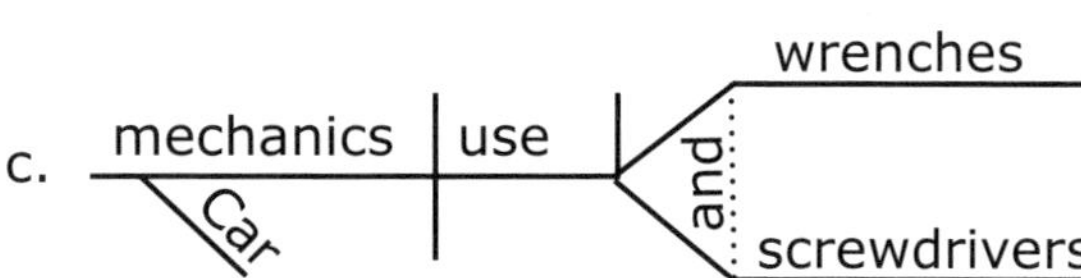

2 a. 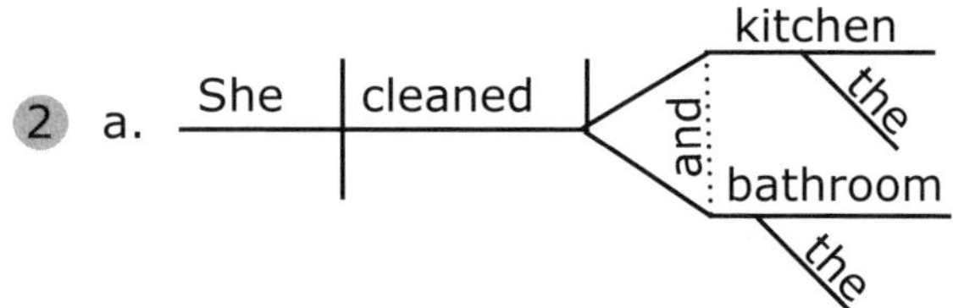

b. 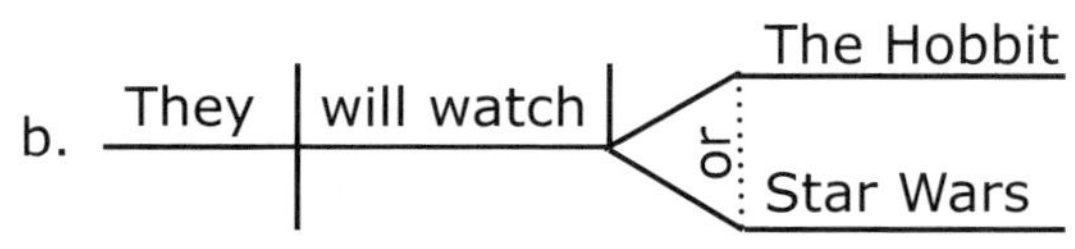

c. 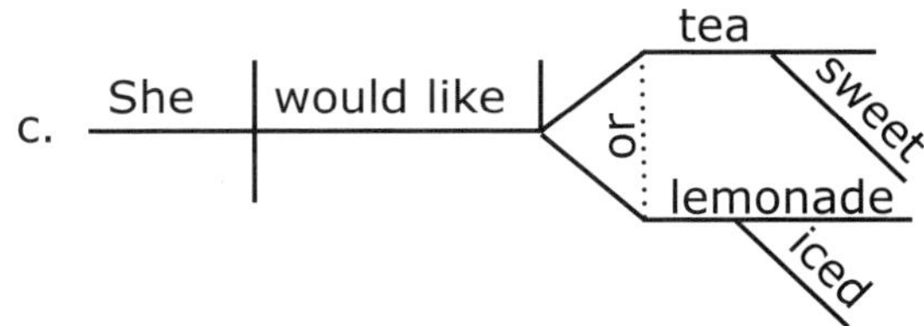

3 Sentences will vary. Examples:

a. He built robots and androids.

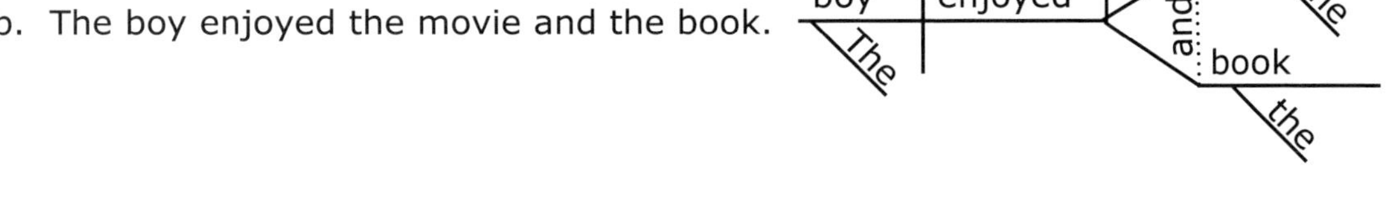

b. The boy enjoyed the movie and the book.

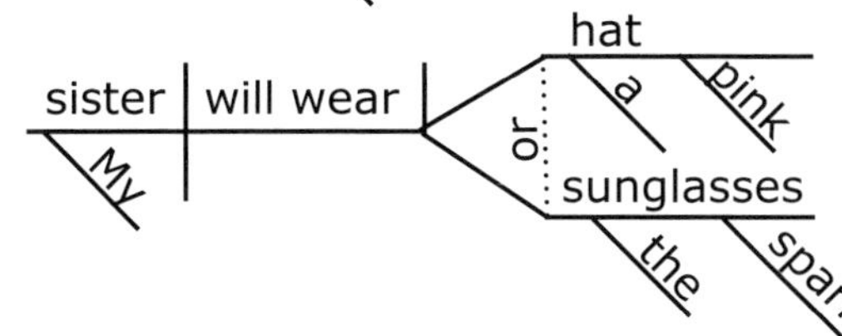

c. My sister will wear a pink hat or the sparkly sunglasses.

4 a. 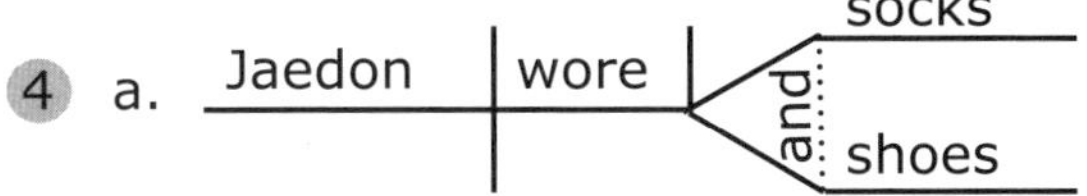

b. 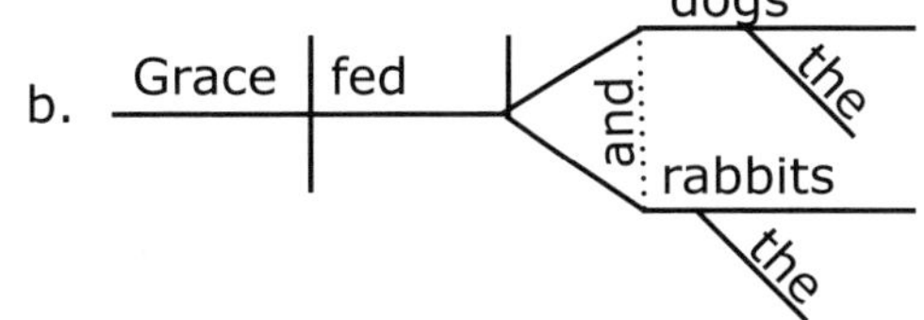

c. 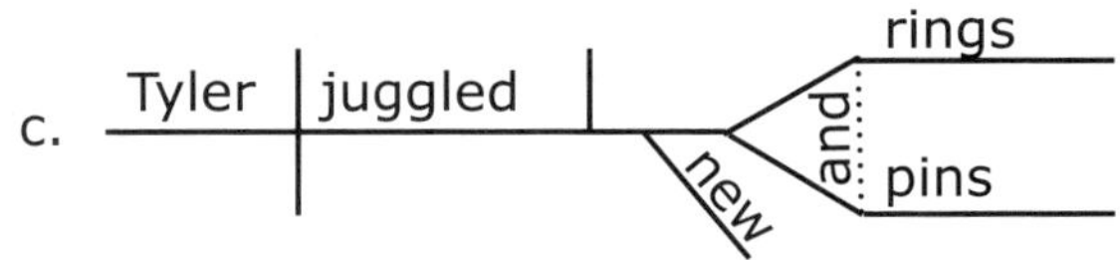

d. 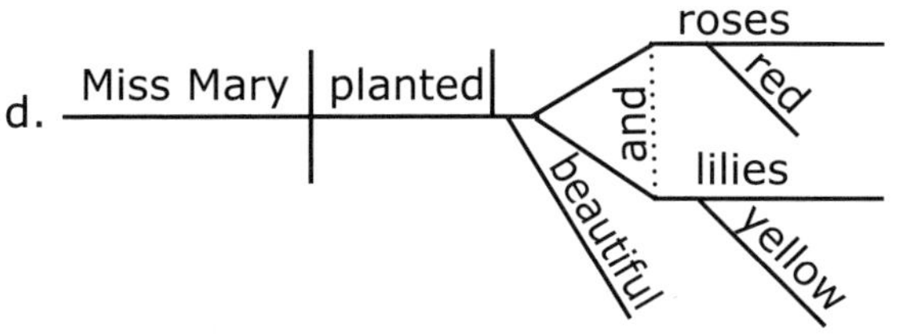

Lesson 12 (pp. 45-48)

1 a. 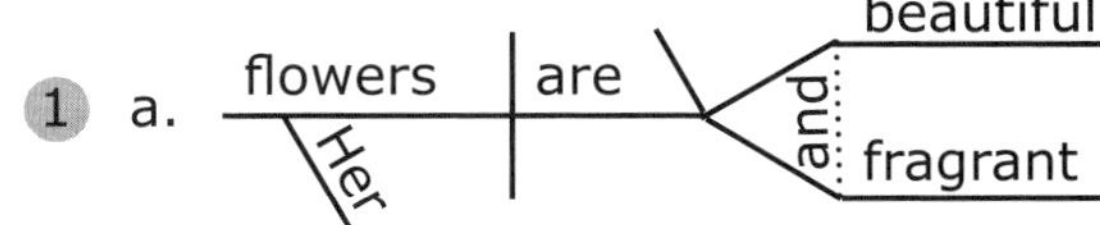

b. 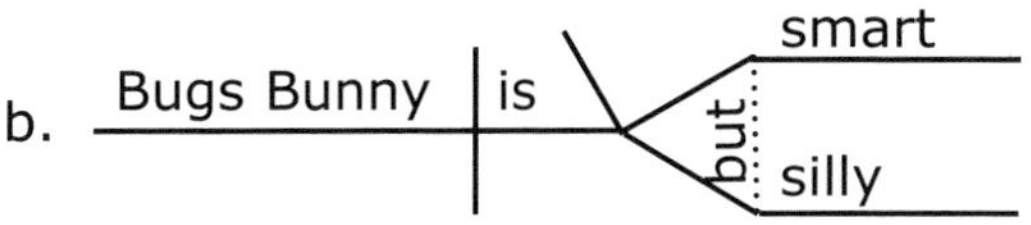

2 a. 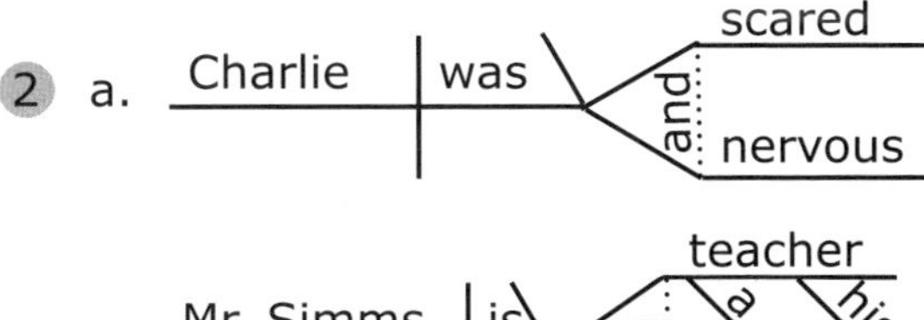

b. 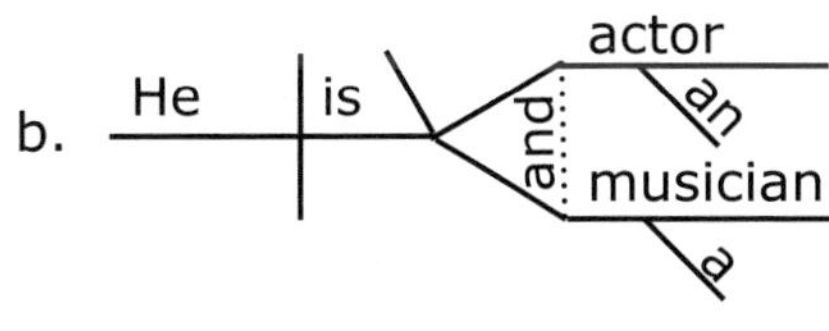

c. 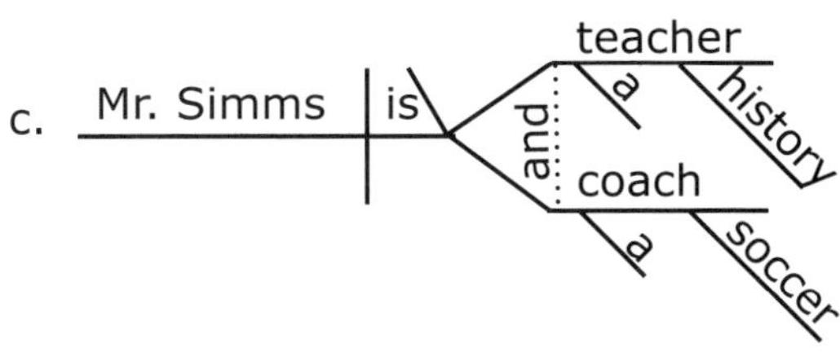

3 Sentences will vary. Examples:

a. Snakes are scaly reptiles and silent predators.

b. That is scary thunder and lightning.

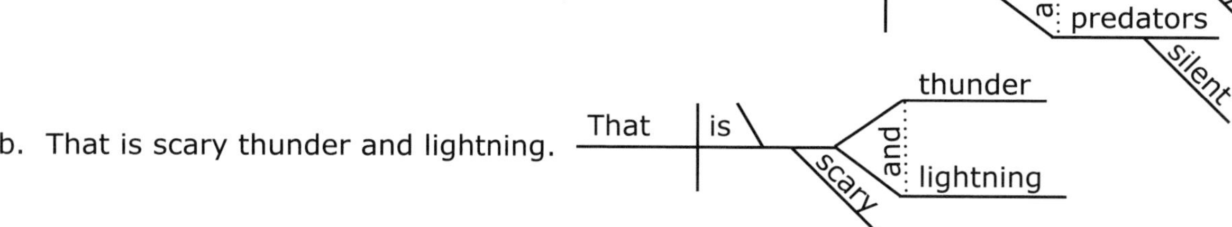

4 a.

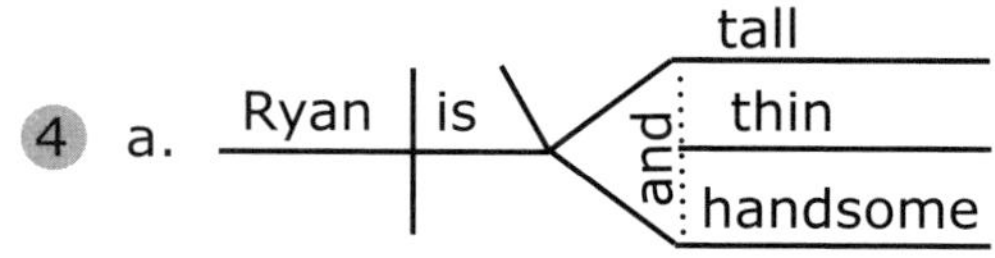

b.

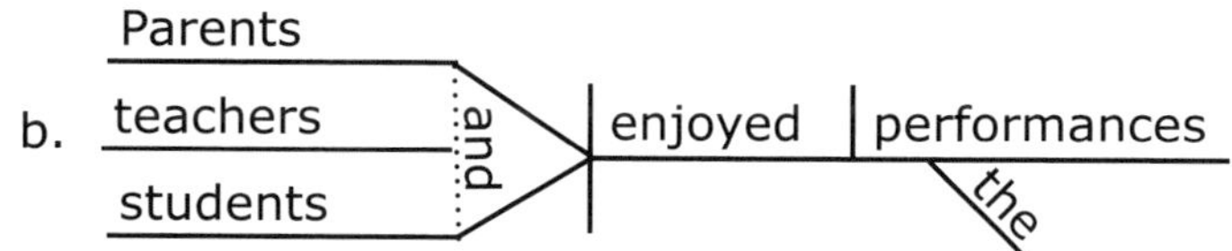

c.

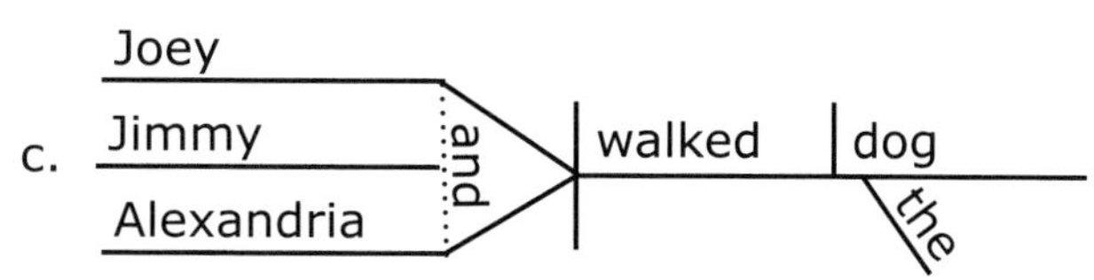

d.

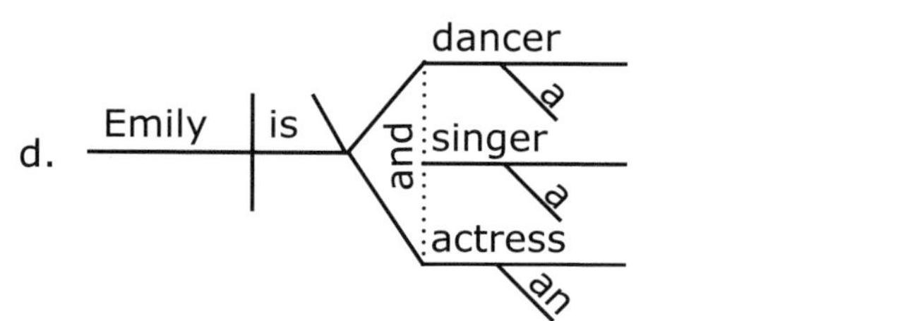

Review (pp. 49-53)

1 President Washington | died

2 Benjamin Franklin | discovered | electricity

3 Johanna Spyri | wrote | Heidi

4 Abraham Lincoln | wore | hat — a, top

5

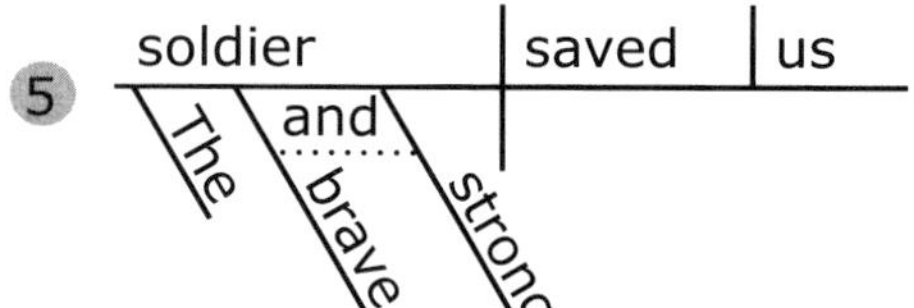

6 kangaroo | bounced — The, baby, joyfully

7

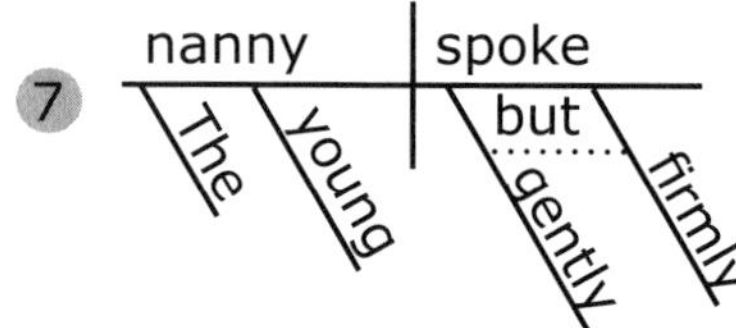

8 Percy Jackson | is \ demi-god — a

9 cousin | is \ she — My

10 Tom Sawyer | was \ mischievous

11

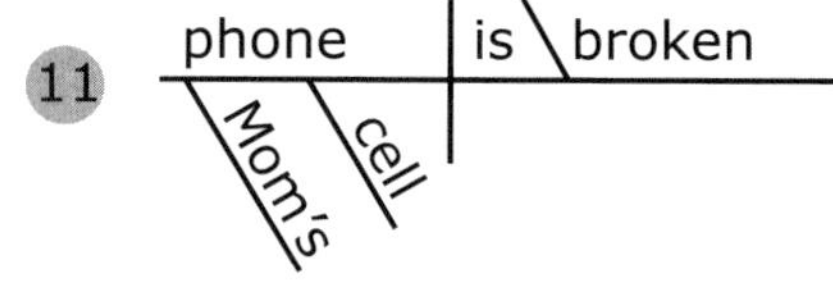

12 shovels | are \ new — The, purple, in, sandbox, the

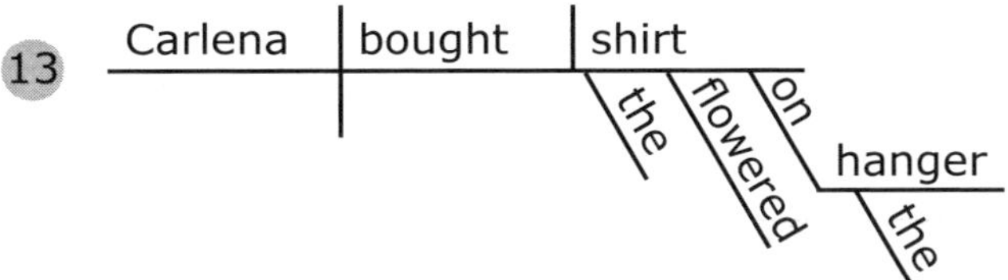
13
Carlena
bought
shirt
the
flowered
on
hanger
the

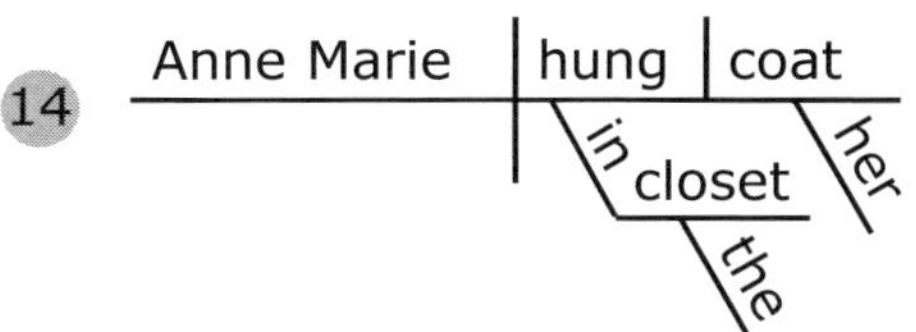
14
Anne Marie
hung
coat
in
closet
the
her

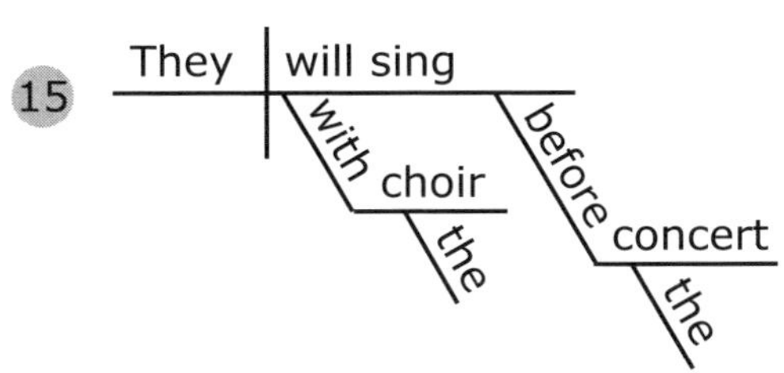
15
They
will sing
with
choir
the
before
concert
the

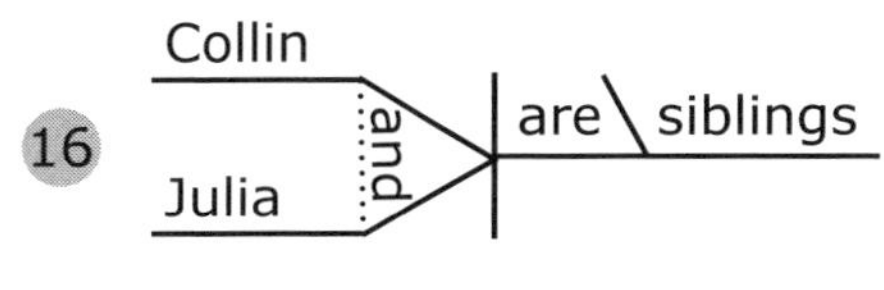
16
Collin
Julia
and
are
siblings

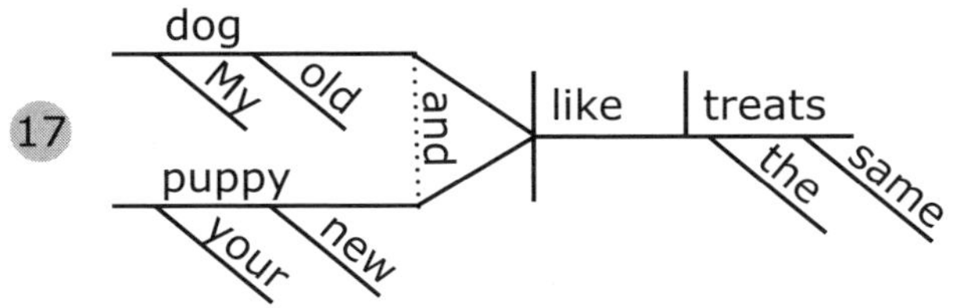
17
dog
My
old
puppy
your
new
and
like
treats
the
same

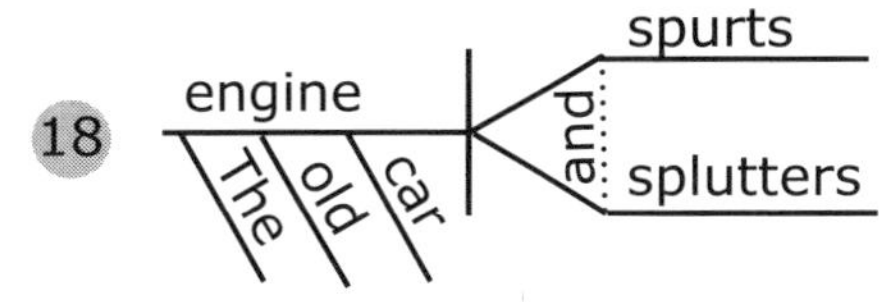
18
engine
The
old
car
and
spurts
splutters

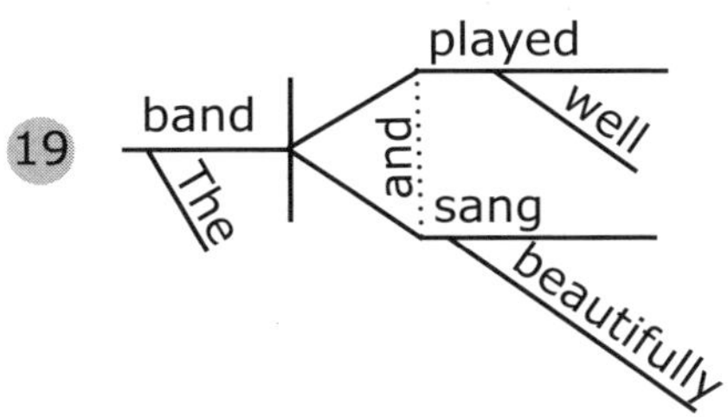
19
band
The
and
played
well
sang
beautifully

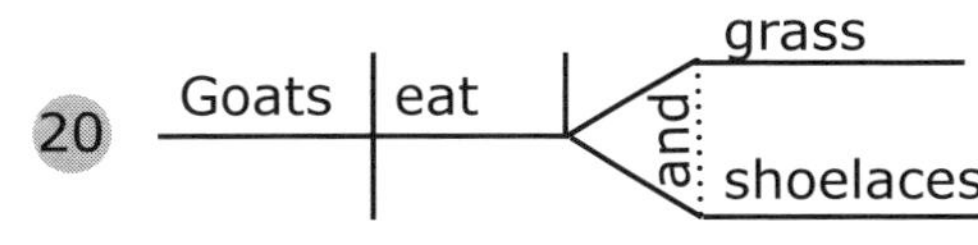
20
Goats
eat
and
grass
shoelaces

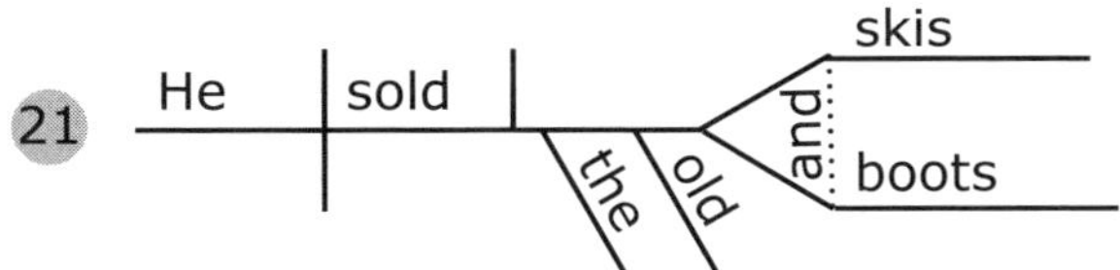
21
He
sold
the
old
and
skis
boots

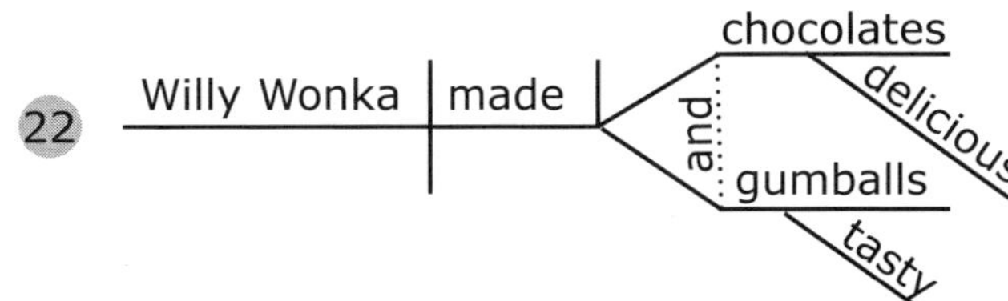
22
Willy Wonka
made
and
chocolates
delicious
gumballs
tasty

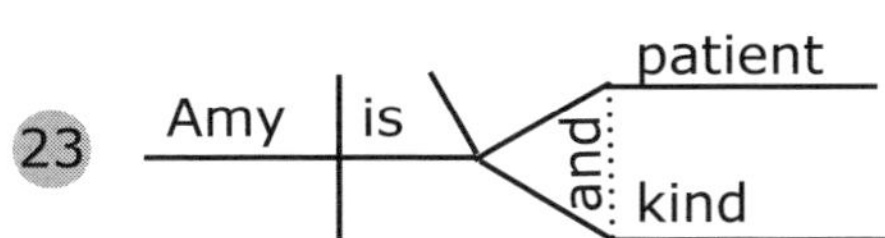
23
Amy
is
and
patient
kind

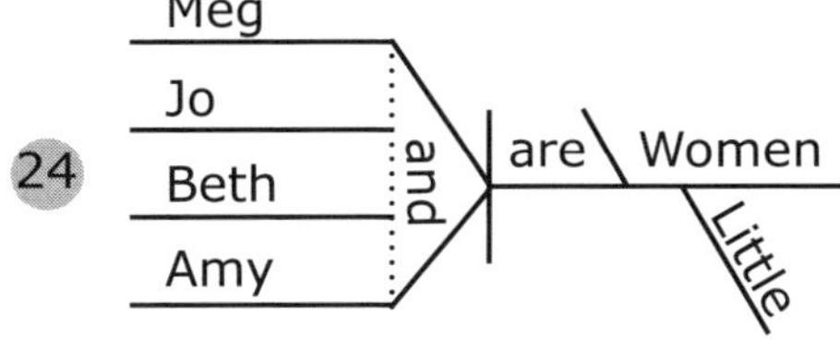
24
Meg
Jo
Beth
Amy
and
are
Women
Little

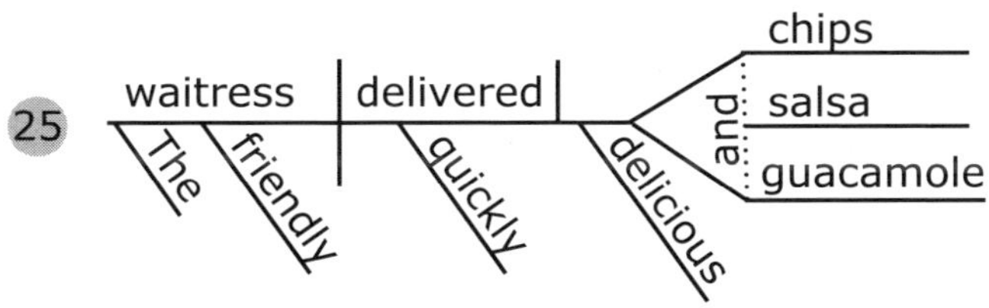
25
waitress
The
friendly
delivered
quickly
delicious
and
chips
salsa
guacamole

Additional Award-Winning Products From The Critical Thinking Co.™

Grades 2-3

Grades 3-4

Grades 4-5

Grades 6-8

Grades 9-12+

Editor in Chief®

Grammar Disasters and Punctuation Faux Pas

- Award Winning
- Full Curriculum
- Test Prep
- Meets State Standards

This highly acclaimed, award-winning series has easy-to-understand lessons, activities, and periodic reviews. *Editor in Chief®* books teach grammar, punctuation, spelling, capitalization, and critical reading in a standards-based thinking approach rather than drill and practice. After a concise lesson that explains and illustrates the mechanics of writing, students carefully analyze and edit stories, letters, and articles that contain mechanical errors. This effective method allows students to gain mastery over concepts that will translate into their own writing. Note: The Level 3 book does not contain content lessons, but rather a grammar guide that covers all the skills used in the book.

- Capitalization
- Adjectives
- Adverbs
- Agreement
- Articles
- Clauses
- Comparisons
- Conjunctions
- Homophones
- Homographs
- Interjections
- Negative Words
- Nouns
- Phrases
- Prepositions
- Pronouns
- Run-On Sentences
- Sentence Fragments
- Verbs
- Confused Word Pairs
- Apostrophes
- Colons
- Comma
- Exclamation Marks
- Hyphens
- Question Marks
- Quotation Marks
- Parenthesis
- Periods
- Semicolons
- Spelling

Awards: Creative Child Magazine Preferred Choice ★ Mom's Choice Awards® Gold medal for Excellence, Best Educational Product ★ Practical Homeschooling Magazine 1st Place Grammar Award ★ Practical Homeschooling Magazine 2nd Place Grammar Award ★ Homeschool.com - Seal of Approval: Recommended Educational Curriculum and Website ★ Practical Homeschooling Magazine, 1st Place Software Award, Thinking/Logic Category ★ Mom's Choice Awards® Gold medal for excellence, best in family-friendly media ★ Practical Homeschooling Magazine 1st Place Interactive Learning Award, Grammar Category ★ Practical Homeschooling Magazine Honorable Mention Reader Award, Vocabulary Category ★ Practical Homeschooling Magazine 2nd Place Interactive Learning Award, Grammar Category ★ Practical Homeschooling Magazine 1st Place Interactive Learning Award, Thinking/Logic Category ★ Recommended Resource for Successful Teaching, Learning® Magazine ★ Practical Homeschooling Magazine Reader Award, Honorable Mention, Grammar category

Also available as software for most phones, tablets, and computers!

iOS  

Review
Lessons 1–6

Read the passage and correct the errors. There are no errors in the picture or caption.

29. The *Titanic*

①	Content
① ②	Capitalization
①	Punctuation
① ②	Spelling
① ②	Noun/Pronoun
① ②	Adjective
①	Adverb

The british ocean liner *Titanic* was a real large ship that was thought to be unsinkable. The Titanic made its first and only voyaje in 1912. It was scheduled to sail from England to New York City. The ship was about 1,600 miles from New York when it collided with an iceburg in the North Atlantic ocean. This collision caused a gash 300 feet long in the ships' hull. It took two hours and forty minutes for the *Titanic* to sink. The worse part of all was that there were not enough lifeboats for everyone on board. Tragically, about 1,400 people died that night. Due to the huge number of lives lost, the sinking of the *Titanic* is considered to be the deadlier peacetime, maritime disaster in modern history. The *Titanic* has undoubtedly become one of the most famous ships in history. His memory is kept alive by numerous books folk songs, movies, exhibits, and memorials.

The *Titanic*, thought to be the safest ship afloat, sank on its first voyage, killing about 1,500 people.

Optional: Use another piece of paper to rewrite the passage without errors.